The New French Gourmet Vegetarian Cookbook

D1571346

The New French Gourmet Vegetarian Cookbook

Rosine Claire

Celestial Arts
Millbrae, California

Copyright © 1975, 1979 by Rosine Claire
CELESTIAL ARTS
231 Adrian Road
Millbrae, California 94030

No part of this book may be reproduced by any mechanical, photographic, or electronic process, or in the form of a phonographic recording, nor may it be stored in a retrieval system, transmitted, or otherwise copied for public or private use without the written permission of the publisher.

Cover Design by Abigail Johnston
Interior Design by Betsy Bruno
Interior gouaches by Catherine Buxhoeveden

First Printing, September 1975
Made in the United States of America

Library of Congress Cataloging in Publication Data

Claire, Rosine, 1911–
    The French gourmet vegetarian cookbook.

    Includes index.
    1. Vegetarianism.   2. Cookery, French.   I. Title.
TX837.C498   641.5'636   75-9086
ISBN 0-89087-058-6-pbk.

3   4   5   6   7   8   —   82   81   80   79

Table of Contents

Before You Begin

Many of the recipes in this book are intended primarily for complete vegetarians; others for those vegetarians who also eat dairy products and eggs. The main purpose of this book is to help people find an easy way to prepare healthy, tasty meals. Being a vegetarian need not be dull. You will learn to prepare delicious soups and salads, appetizing entrees and delectable desserts using greens, fruits, grains, roots, and last but not least, nuts and seeds!

If you consume raw or slightly cooked food you need not eat large quantities. It is not only economical but helps to prevent overeating. If you choose wholesome food (without chemical additives) you will find it both satisfying and nourishing.

Selection and Preparation

The first step is to buy organically grown, unsprayed fruits and vegetables. The ideal situation would be to grow them in your own garden. But if that is not convenient and you cannot find organically grown vegetables and fruits, my advice is to wash them carefully since cooking *does not* remove the harmful effect of spraying. There are some liquid concentrates available in health food stores which are effective. Use them in small quantities mixed with water as directed. If you have nothing special on hand use vinegar, lemon juice or bicarbonate of soda, mixing one tablespoon to one quart of water.

1

Fresh fruits and vegetables are preferable in all instances. When only the frozen varieties are available be certain to use only those that are packaged without additives or sugar syrup.

Cookware

Most of our recipes suggest cooking vegetables in their own juice, with very little water. You should use steel cookware, with a tight fitting lid. The old fashioned Dutch oven is also good. Stainless steel pots are easy to clean. For casseroles, Pyrex and Corningware are excellent. *Do not use aluminum!*

Water

Unfortunately, water taken from the tap is no longer very suitable. See *The Vegetarian Way of Life* by Hans Holzer, 1973, Pyramid Publications. It would be ideal, of course, to have your own well. The next best alternative is spring water, available in most grocery stores.

Oils

I would advise the use of only cold pressed oils, without chemical additives, for cooking and making sauces. Sunflower and safflower seed oils, which are unsaturated fatty acid, sesame seed oil, tasty olive oil, peanut oil, light corn oil for cooking, walnut, almond and apricot kernel oil are all delicious. As you can see there is a large choice of oils to mix with your salads and vegetables.

Butter

If you do not wish to use real butter, or are a strict vegetarian, some health food stores carry vegetable butter made from soy beans. In addition, you will find delicious almond, cashew or peanut butter available or you can make your own nut butter at home. Homemade nut butter should be made in small amounts of fresh, raw, unsalted nuts, and be kept in the refrigerator. Grind a cupful of almonds, cashews, or peanuts etc., to a flour consistency. Put it in a bowl, adding enough oil and water to blend the mixture into a thick paste. Add salt if desired.

Herbs

I use many herbs in my recipes. Not only do they add flavor to a dish, but each herb has a special medicinal quality. For example, sage is cleansing, marjoram calming, savory aids digestion, thyme is antibiotic and parsley contains vitamin A. Use them freely. Even though you don't have a garden, you can grow herbs on your window sill. There are herb kits on the market and if you have a sunny window and a green thumb it is a lot of fun.

Salt

You will notice that I often don't mention salt in the recipes, because one should season to one's own taste. Moreover, I prefer to use sea salt or sea kelp which you will find in your health food store. Always add the salt when the food is almost done cooking.

Sugar

By sugar I mean raw sugar, honey or maple syrup.

ONE

Fruits

Fruits are one of the most natural foods. They are abundant and offer a wide variety of choice. They contain essential vitamins and glucose, a form of sugar easily assimilated by the body. It is preferable to eat fruit alone, during the day or before meals because fruits are digested very fast. If consumed after a heavy meal they can cause stomach upset.

The most nutritious way to eat fruit is raw, with the skin on. If they have been sprayed they should be washed thoroughly. Fruits may be made into a compote with a little raw sugar, honey or maple syrup added, or into preserves or jelly. But remember, cooking always destroys some of the delicate vitamins and enzymes.

I suggest eating plenty of fresh fruits especially when they are in season. Your body will be cleansed by strawberries in the spring, peaches in summer, and grapes in the fall.

You can freeze the summer fruits, such as peaches, apricots, cherries, melons and berries to keep them available all year round. If possible buy baskets of fruit in the country when they are less expensive and freeze them. Frozen foods retain most of their nutritive qualities which makes freezing the best method of preserving food.

Do work rapidly. As soon as possible after buying fruits, wash them in cold water to keep them firm. Any water on the fruit will freeze, so be sure to use pure water. Fruits can be frozen without sugar syrup; just put them in cellophane bags and close tight.

If you prefer to freeze them in sugar syrup or honey syrup, prepare it by cooking sugar or honey in water using one part sugar or honey to three parts water. Cool and pour over the fruit. Use special freezer containers for storage. With peaches, apricots and melons, peel and slice quickly. Put in container and pour syrup over them to within one inch of the top of the container. Fruits should be fully covered by the syrup and sealed tight.

Try these fruit suggestions for lunch or a light dinner.

Melon Surprise

One half a small cantaloupe per person. Open cantaloupe in half, remove seeds from center and fill with a mixture of blueberries and raspberries soaked in honey. Top with fruit ice cream or sherbet.

Peaches Chantilly

Peel and slice peaches. Arrange slices around individual plates. Fill the center with pitted cherries sweetened with honey. Top with whipped cream.

Banana Split

Split bananas and arrange in circles on plates. Fill the center with blueberries sweetened with honey. Top with sour cream and walnuts.

Nectar Fruit Salad

1 pint fresh strawberries
1 pint fresh raspberries
1 pint blueberries
2 peaches, sliced
2 tablespoons pineapple
  juice

1 orange peeled and sliced
1 can unsweetened
  pineapple,
  drained and sliced
3 tablespoons honey

Combine all ingredients and mix well. Sprinkle with finely chopped filberts and chill. Serves six.

All Fruits Breakfast

1 fresh apple, chopped
1 ounce raisins
2 dates, minced
2 prunes, soaked overnight

1 tablespoon of coconut meal
1 banana, sliced
2 tablespoons cream
apple or pineapple juice
  to moisten

Mix ingredients together, moistening with either apple or pineapple juice. Place mixture in center of serving plate and surround with banana slices. Top with cream and a few pine nuts (pignoli). Serves two.

Winter Party Salad

1 fresh pineapple,
  cleaned and diced
2 apples, peeled and cut
  into thin slices
1 pear, peeled and cut
  into thin slices

¼ cup raisins
¼ cup pine nuts
1 banana, sliced
3 tablespoons apple juice
2 tablespoons maple syrup
3 dates, chopped

Combine all ingredients and chill. Serves six.

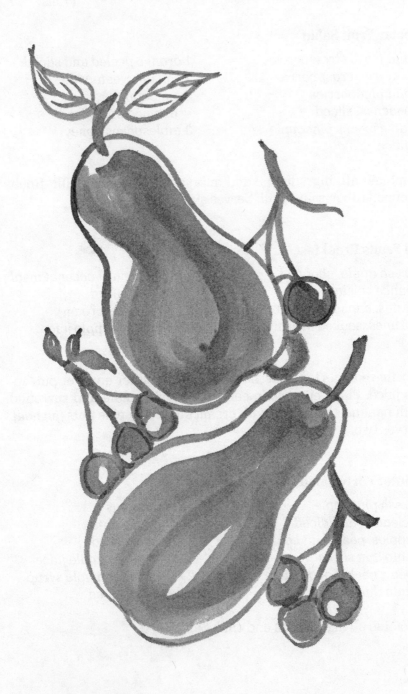

TWO

Dried Fruits

Dried fruits make delicious compotes. They can be prepared in two ways. To cook them, mix the fruits you like and cover with cold water. Add a small amount of sugar, and simmer on very low heat. Serve cold. Uncooked, cover the mixture of dried fruit with hot water, and let it stand overnight or at least several hours. Serve cold.

Greek Prunes (Pruneaux à la Grecque)

1 pound large prunes
juice of one orange
¼ cup red wine

2 tablespoons raw sugar
5 cloves
water to cover the prunes

Combine ingredients and cook over low heat for about 1 hour. Add more water if necessary. Refrigerate. Serves four.

Almond Apricots (Abricots aux Amandes)

1 pound dried apricots   ¼ pound raisins
¼ pound blanched almonds   3 tablespoons sugar or honey

Combine all ingredients except almonds, cover with cold water and simmer over low heat for one hour. Serve warm or cold. Serves four.

Dried Fruit Medley

½ pound Italian figs   few lemon peels
½ pound raisins   2 ounces pine nuts
½ pound prunes   few almonds
¼ pound dried apples   few walnuts

Combine ingredients except the nuts, in saucepan. Cover with cold water and simmer on low heat about one to one and one-half hours. Ten minutes before the end of cooking add one tablespoon of maple syrup or honey. It is not necessary to add sugar, because the figs are very sweet. Add nuts and serve cold.

THREE

Salads

Salads are an important part of vegetarian fare. Try to eat one daily. Greens are the basis for nearly all salads and contain chlorophyll as well as vitamins and minerals. There are many different greens on the market. At the top of the list I would suggest Boston (or butter) lettuce, Bibb lettuce and romaine; then escarole, curly chicory and endive. Iceberg lettuce is not as desirable from a nutritional standpoint. Watercress is very important for its cleansing value. Then come spinach, Chinese and other cabbages, celery tops and beet tops.

Wash all greens carefully in cold water and if they have been chemically sprayed use an organic cleansing agent. Drain in a French salad basket or dry them in a towel. Keep cold until served.

Some gourmets prefer a wooden salad bowl which can be wiped clean after each use instead of washing. A wooden salad fork and spoon are also better for tossing salads.

Tossed Salad

1 small head of Boston (or butter) lettuce	½ head escarole
½ head romaine lettuce	1 clove garlic, chopped
	1 onion, chopped

Tear lettuce, add onion and garlic and toss with choice of dressing. Serve with Vinaigrette (page 26), or French Dressing (page 27). Serves six.

Salad of the Auvergne Region

This salad is a meal in itself. My grandmother used to make it on hot summer days. It is pleasant to eat with fruit for dessert.

1 large head curly chicory	French Dressing (page 27).
2 scallions, chopped fine	1 teaspoon fresh chervil
4 hard boiled eggs	1 teaspoon of parsley
4 whole beets, cooked	4 cloves garlic
Mustard Sauce (page 36)	8 slices of French bread

Mix chicory, scallions and beets. Add a Mustard Sauce or French Dressing and toss well. Cut eggs in half, placing them around sides of the bowl. Garnish with chopped herbs. Clean the garlic and cut each clove in half. Rub each slice of French bread with garlic. Serves four.

French Salad

In France this salad is frequently served after the main course, just before the cheese.

1 head of Boston (butter) or
   romaine lettuce
1 clove of garlic

1 onion, minced
1 teaspoon fresh chervil
1 teaspoon fresh parsley

Cut lettuce into sections, one per serving. Sprinkle with mixture of other ingredients. Top with Vinaigrette (page 26). Serves four to six.

Salade Parisienne

2 bunches watercress, cut
1 small onion, chopped
2 endive, cut lengthwise

¼ pound raw mushrooms,
   sliced

Mix together watercress, onion, endive and mushrooms. Drizzle with Mustard Sauce. (page 36). Since watercress has a nippy flavor it is not necessary to add garlic or other herbs.

Dandelion Salad

Choose young dandelion leaves. Wash thoroughly and dry on absorbent towel. Mix with a few leaves of Bibb lettuce, chopped scallions and whole cooked beets. Top with your favorite dressing.

Greek Salad (Salade à la Grecque)

½ cup brown rice   1 tablespoon honey
Dressing: Beat together   1 tablespoon cider vinegar
½ pint plain yogurt

Cook rice, cool, and mix with dressing.

8 ounces spinach   ½ pound feta cheese
2 scallions, chopped   ½ cup black olives,
2 tomatoes, cut in pieces   pitted and sliced
                                    juice of one lemon

Wash spinach and cut finely. Add scallions, tomatoes, small pieces of feta cheese and olives. Sprinkle with lemon juice and more dressing if desired. Serve with rice. Serves four.

Hollywood Salad

¼ pound spinach leaves, cut   ¼ pound mushrooms, sliced
2 carrots, grated   1 tablespoon sunflower
Greek feta cheese, diced   seeds
1 tablespoon sprouted grains

Combine ingredients. Top with Creole Dressing (page 26). Serves four to six.

Potpourri Salad

1 head Boston
   (butter) lettuce
few leaves spinach
¼ green pepper, chopped
1 onion, chopped
½ avocado, sliced

2 leaves endive
1 bunch watercress
½ cucumber, sliced
1 tomato, sliced (in season)
few nuts, and sunflower
   seeds

Add anything you like to potpourri. Top with your favorite dressing. Serves six to eight.

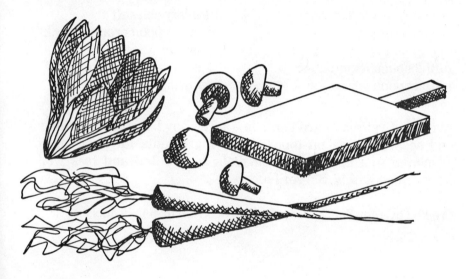

Summer Salad

1 head Boston
   (butter) lettuce
2 leaves endive
1 cup alfalfa sprouts
1 bunch radishes

2 tomatoes, quartered
1 green pepper,
   sliced into rings
1 bunch scallions

Wash and prepare ingredients for individual salad bowls. Line each with leaves of Boston lettuce. Cover with sliced endive and then the sprouts and cucumber, radishes and tomatoes, finishing with rings of green pepper. Arrange scallions around sides of bowl. Top with Honey Lemon Dressing (page 27). Serves four to six.

Hot Spinach Salad

1 pound fresh spinach
   leaves, torn to
   salad size
3 ounces onions, finely sliced
3 ounces mushrooms, finely
   sliced
3 hard-boiled eggs, quartered

6 whole cherry tomatoes
1 ounce sesame seeds,
   toasted

1 cup garlic croutons
   (optional)

Dressing:
½ cup rice wine vinegar
½ cup water
½ cup honey
1 tablespoon lemon juice
1 tablespoon soy sauce

1 tablespoon salt
½ tablespoon ground black
   pepper
½ tablespoon mustard
   powder

Arrange first five ingredients in a large bowl. Sprinkle croutons and sesame seeds on top. Mix all ingredients for dressing in saucepan and bring to a boil. Pour over salad and toss well. Serve immediately. Serves four.

Created by Tony Santa Elena, Jr., The Good Earth, San Francisco.

Vitality Salad

few leaves Boston
   (butter) lettuce
few leaves romaine lettuce
few leaves escarole
1 beet, grated
2 tomatoes, sliced or
   mushrooms, sliced
1 carrot, grated

few pieces of blue cheese or
   Greek feta
1 tablespoon sunflower meal
1 tablespoon sesame meal
2 tablespoons sprouted
   alfalfa
1 onion, chopped
1 clove garlic
1 hard-boiled egg, sliced

Mix ingredients together. Top with Avocado Dressing (page 25). A meal in itself. Serves four.

Coleslaw Naturel

½ head crisp, fresh
  young cabbage
½ cup green pepper
½ tablespoon fresh ground
  dill seeds

sea salt
paprika
½ cup grated carrots
½ teaspoon caraway seeds

Grate or chop the cabbage as fine as you like. Add carrot and green pepper, mixing well. Add Mustard Sauce (page 36) or Mayonnaise (page 28). Serves four.

Cucumbers à la Polonaise

2 cucumbers, thinly sliced
½ cup sour cream
salt
paprika

2 tablespoons fresh chives,
  chopped
1 tablespoon fresh dill,
  chopped

Mix sour cream with the sliced cucumber. Season to taste and sprinkle top with the herbs and paprika.

Cucumbers à la Française

Peel cucumber and slice thin. Place in a dish and sprinkle generously with sea salt. Let stand a moment to disgorge. This will make the cucumber more digestible. Then, wash cucumber in cold water, drain and dry in a towel. Place in a salad bowl and pour on Vinaigrette (page 26). Top with dill and parsley. Serves two to four.

Salad Combinations

Grated carrot, raisins and pine nuts. Serve with Mayonnaise (page 28).

Chopped red cabbage, celery and onion. Serve with French Dressing (page 27).

Sliced tomatoes and red onion with chopped fresh basil. Top with Vinaigrette (page 26).

Raw cauliflower flowerets, with black olives. Serve with Mayonnaise (page 28).

Cooked cauliflower, with chopped onions and parsley. Serve with Vinaigrette (page 26).

Raw sauerkraut with black olives. Serve with Honey Lemon Dressing (page 27).

Cooked fresh string beans with chopped shallots, garlic and parsley. Serve with Vinaigrette (page 26) or French Dressing (page 27).

Raw young peas, with chopped celery, scallions, and slice of avocado. Serve with Mayonnaise (page 28).

Radishes. Wash and trim off tops and tails. Make into lilies by using a small knife to slit the radish down from the tail end, six times to form petals. Soak in cold water to open. Serve with peanut butter or sweet butter.

Russian Salad

1 pound fresh string beans,
  cooked and diced
1 pound fresh baby lima
  beans, cooked
1 pound fresh small peas,
  cooked
1 small bunch broccoli,
  cooked and cut

3 carrots, cooked and sliced
3 beets, cooked and sliced
2 stalks raw celery, chopped
1 large onion
2 cloves garlic, chopped
¼ cup chopped parsley

Mix well. Top with Rosine's Dressing (page 29). Serves eight to ten.

Potato Salad

6 medium potatoes
½ cup onion or scallions,
   chopped
½ cup celery, chopped

3 tablespoons oil
2 tablespoons vinegar
juice of one lemon

Boil potatoes in their skins. Peel and cube while still warm. Place into salad bowl and combine with onions and celery. Sprinkle with three tablespoons of warm water and add oil, vinegar, and lemon juice. Cool and taste. It may be necessary to add more oil or vinegar. Top with parsley. Serves six to eight.

Variation: Potato salad may be made by substituting ½ cup Mayonnaise for oil, vinegar and lemon.

Lentil Salad

1 pound lentils, sorted and
   washed
5 cups water
1 bay leaf
sea salt
2 onions stuck with
   2 whole cloves each
½ cup olive or peanut oil
1 teaspoon mustard

1 teaspoon honey
¼ cup apple cider vinegar
   or lemon juice
paprika
1 clove garlic
1 stalk celery, chopped
2 scallions, chopped
3 teaspoons parsley,
   chopped

Place the lentils in cold water and add bay leaf, salt and onions in the cookware. Bring to a boil, cover and simmer for thirty minutes or until lentils are tender but not overcooked. Drain off excess liquid. Remove onions and bay leaf and place lentils in a salad bowl. Meanwhile, make sauce by combining the oil, mustard, honey, vinegar or lemon juice, sea salt and paprika to taste. Mix thoroughly and pour over the hot lentils. When cool add chopped garlic, celery, scallions and parsley. Chill. Serves about ten.

Morning Salad

leaves of Boston (butter) or
    Bibb lettuce
alfalfa sprouts

4 dried Elberta peaches
8 dried apricots

Soak dried fruits in water for 24 hours before use. Spread lettuce leaves on the plates. Place sprouts on each leaf and the chopped fruits on top, allowing the juice from the fruits to scatter over the leaves. Top with honey and sour cream. Serves four.

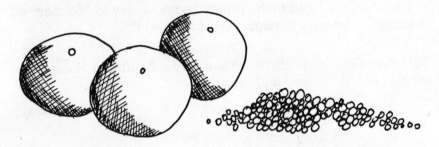

Fantasia Salad

leaves of Boston (butter) lettuce
2 grapefruit

4 oranges
blueberries or raspberries

Peel and section grapefruit and oranges. Arrange the lettuce leaves on 4 plates and place slices of grapefruit and oranges alternately to form a ring. Heap berries in center. Top with honey. Serves four.

Molded Salad

2 pints of vegetable or
    tomato juice
4 teaspoons agar-agar flakes
1 carrot, chopped
1 celery stalk, chopped

1 onion, chopped
1 teaspoon dried basil
1 teaspoon tarragon
4 black olives, sliced
juice of one lemon

Sprinkle agar-agar flakes in juice and boil for 5 minutes. Add all other ingredients and mix thoroughly. Pour into wet mold and chill until firm. Unmold and serve with slice of lemon. Serves four to six.

Far Eastern Vegetable Curry Salad Mold

1 cup baby peas,
  cooked and chilled
1 cup long grain rice,
  cooked and chilled
½ cup water chestnuts,
  chopped
½ cup onions, minced
½ cup raisins

1 ounce red ginger, pickled,
  cut in long, thin strips
½ cup mayonnaise
1 tablespoon curry powder
1 tablespoon honey
1 tablespoon soy sauce
1 tablespoon rice wine

Mix all ingredients thoroughly. On a plate layered with lettuce, form a cone-shaped mound. Garnish with tomato slices. Chill for about one hour. Serves four.

Created by Tony Santa Elena, Jr., The Good Earth, San Francisco.

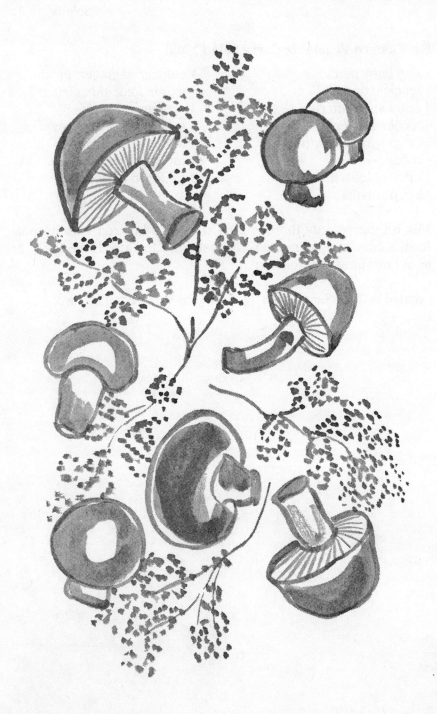

FOUR

Raw Appetizers (Crudités)

Avocado Vie Claire

2 medium avocados
¼ cup chopped dill and
    parsley

juice of one lemon
8 mushrooms
Mustard Sauce (page 36)

Cut the avocados in half. Pour lemon juice over them to keep from turning black. Scoop out and chop pulp and mushrooms together. Mix in Mustard Sauce. Fill avocado shells. Sprinkle with dill and parsley. Serves four.

Avocado Flowers

Peel and slice avocado lengthwise in eighths. Arrange slices in a ring on a bed of lettuce leaves on a plate. Fill center with yogurt dip (page 32). Sprinkle with lemon juice. One per serving.

Tomatoes Vie Claire

2 large tomatoes
4 black olives

6 mushrooms
4 teaspoons parsley
Mustard Sauce (page 36)

Cut the tomatoes in half. Scoop out tomato pulp and chop the pulp and mushrooms together. Mix in Mustard Sauce. Fill the tomato halves. Sprinkle with parsley. Garnish with an olive. Serves four.

Mushrooms in Green Sauce

1 tablespoon almond or
    cashew butter
3 tablespoons water
¼ tablespoon sea salt
¼ teaspoon nutmeg
3 to 4 tablespoons olive oil

juice of one lemon
½ cup parsley, chopped
chervil and dill
a few black olives
½ pound mushrooms

Dilute the nut butter in the water. Add salt and nutmeg. Pour the oil slowly and stir to the consistency of a mayonnaise. Add the lemon juice slowly and then the herbs. Put the sliced mushrooms onto a plate and pour the sauce over them. Garnish with black olives. Serves four.

FIVE

Dressings for Salads and Raw Vegetables

Avocado Dressing

The word avocado comes from the Nahuatlan word *ahuacatl.* The Nahuatls were but one of numerous Indian tribes discovered in Mexico and Central America by the Spanish in the sixteenth century.

A life-giving food, the avocado is high in calories. However, it replaces oil and eggs for people who don't eat eggs and it is an excellent substitute for mayonnaise.

1 avocado	*1 teaspoon mustard*
1 large lemon	*2 teaspoons honey*
½ cup water or pineapple juice	

Mix all ingredients in the blender for 1 minute. Serve on green salads, vegetables, or fruits.

Creole Dressing

½ cup avocado oil
1 cup tomato juice
2 teaspoons honey
1 teaspoon paprika
1 tablespoon vegetable broth
   in powdered form

juice of 2 lemons or
   2 tablespoons cider
   vinegar
½ cup olive oil
1 onion, chopped fine
1 clove garlic, chopped
salt

Combine all ingredients and mix together in blender for several minutes. Refrigerate in a jar or bottle. Shake well before using. Creole Dressing is especially good on a tossed salad.

French Vinaigrette

6 tablespoons olive oil
2 tablespoons wine or
   cider vinegar

½ teaspoon tarragon leaves
salt and pepper
garlic powder

Combine ingredients and mix thoroughly.

Spanish Style Vinaigrette

6 tablespoons olive oil
1 teaspoon sugar
¼ of a large red onion,
   chopped fine

2 tablespoons wine vinegar
salt, pepper

Mix well. Serve with cold asparagus, leeks or artichokes.

French Dressing

1 cup peanut oil
1 teaspoon honey
1 teaspoon tomato puree

½ cup cider vinegar
1 teaspoon mustard
salt, pepper

Place all ingredients in a jar and shake well. Refrigerate. Very good with almost every salad.

Honey Lemon Dressing

½ cup safflower oil
1 clove fresh garlic, chopped
juice of 2 lemons

½ cup olive oil
1 tablespoon honey

Place all ingredients in a bottle and shake well, or mix in blender for a few minutes. This dressing will keep several days in refrigerator. Serve with Summer Salad (page 15) or raw vegetable plates.

Mayonnaise

It is said while the Marshal of Richelieu was with his French troops at the gates of Port Mahon, (Baleares, 1756) his cook made a sauce with oil, eggs and lemon which became so popular they brought the recipe back to France. Later the name of "mahonnaise" was changed to "mayonnaise."

Natural Mayonnaise Dressing

1 teaspoon mustard
¼ cup nut butter
¼ teaspoon celery powder
½ cup sunflower oil

¼ cup lemon juice
¼ teaspoon paprika
¼ teaspoon garlic powder
salt to taste

Mix mustard and nut butter. Blend with the oil, adding lemon juice slowly. Add seasonings and blend thoroughly. Will keep several days in refrigerator.

Mayonnaise (Egg)

1 egg yolk
1 teaspoon mustard
1 teaspoon honey

salt and pepper
½ cup sunflower oil
1 tablespoon cider vinegar
   or juice of a large lemon

Mix the egg yolk with mustard, honey, salt and pepper. Measure the oil and add it drop by drop, beating constantly with egg beater or in the blender. When the mayonnaise starts to thicken, the oil may be added more quickly. When thick, add vinegar or lemon. Store in refrigerator.

Roquefort Dressing

2 ounces Roquefort cheese,
   at room temperature
½ cup milk

1 tablespoon sour cream
juice of one lemon

Crush Roquefort. Add milk and stir until creamy and smooth. Add sour cream and lemon juice and mix well. Will keep in refrigerator several days. Serve with tossed salad.

Rosine's Dressing

2 cloves fresh garlic
½ teaspoon dried basil
1 teaspoon tarragon
½ teaspoon dried dill
sea salt and paprika
1 tablespoon French
    mustard

2 tablespoons honey
3 tablespoons spring water
½ cup sunflower oil
½ cup olive oil
2 tablespoons cider vinegar
juice of 2 lemons

Mix garlic, herbs, seasoning, mustard, honey and water in blender for several seconds. Add oils, lemon and vinegar and blend for a few minutes more.

If a blender is not available, combine chopped garlic and herbs. Mix mustard and honey in water and pour in the herbal mixture and seasonings. Slowly add the oils, stirring constantly. Add lemon and vinegar. Pour mixture into a bottle and shake vigorously. Refrigerate. Shake well before each use. This dressing will keep a long time in refrigerator. It is exceptionally good on vegetable salads.

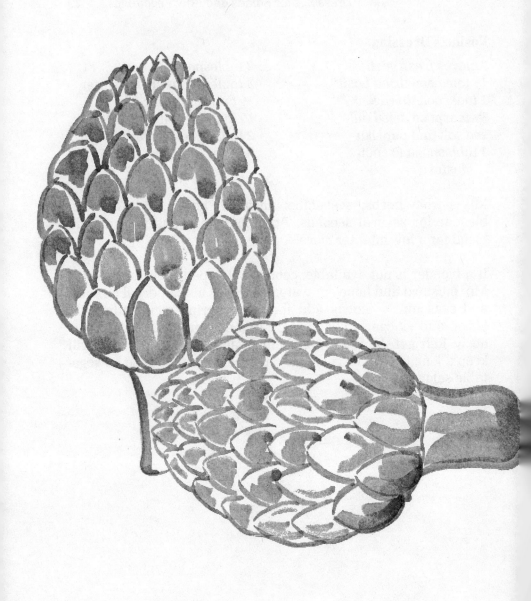

SIX

Spreads and Dips

Blue Cheese Spread

4 tablespoons sour cream
8 ounces cream cheese at
    room temperature

5 ounces blue cheese at room
    temperature
chives

Mash and blend cheeses. Slowly add cream and beat mixture until smooth. Add more cream or milk as necessary. Garnish with fresh, chopped chives. Will keep one week in refrigerator. Serve on celery or crackers.

Danny's Dip

1 pint sour cream
5 tablespoons vegetable
    broth in powdered form
1 teaspoon minced chives

1 teaspoon tarragon
½ teaspoon garlic powder
1 teaspoon parsley, chopped
½ teaspoon paprika

Mix sour cream with the powdered broth and blend until smooth. Add herbs and paprika. Salt is not necessary because broth is already salted. Will keep in refrigerator for several days. Serve on crackers or whole grain bread.

Yogurt Dip

1 pint fresh cottage cheese
1 pint yogurt

chives, chopped
chervil or parsley, chopped
paprika

Mix together cottage cheese and yogurt. Add chopped chives, chervil or parsley. Sprinkle with paprika. Serve immediately. Especially good on avocado or fresh berries.

Sunflower Dip

1 pint yogurt
2 tablespoons chives,
  chopped
½ teaspoon of vegetable salt

1 cup sunflower meal
1 tablespoon parsley,
  chopped

Blend yogurt and meal. Add herbs and top with paprika. Prepare shortly before serving. Tasty with raw vegetables.

Walnut Spread

3 ounces cream cheese
3 tablespoons milk

4 ounces walnuts, chopped
fine

Beat cream cheese with milk. Blend in the walnuts. Especially delicious on dark rye bread.

Sunny Spread

4 ounces sunflower seed butter
4 ounces sesame seed butter

⅔ cup spring water
4 teaspoons sesame seeds

Blend the butter and water together to form a spread. Add more water if necessary to bring to spread consistency. Top with sesame seeds. Serve as a dip with fresh celery or carrot sticks. Delicious on pumpernickel slices.

SEVEN

Sauces

Carob Sauce

Carob beans come from the caroba tree. They have a natural sweetness and may replace cocoa and chocolate in recipes. Available in health food stores.

4 tablespoons carob powder
2 tablespoons honey
1 teaspoon vanilla

1 tablespoon sweet butter
1 cup milk

Mix all ingredients together in saucepan and cook over low heat, stirring constantly until thickened. Serve hot or cold. Serves four.

Custard Sauce

1 pint milk
3 eggs, beaten

2 tablespoons sugar
1 teaspoon vanilla

Warm the milk and pour it over the beaten eggs. Return to pan and add sugar. Reheat gently until the mixture thickens, stirring constantly. Do not boil. Remove from heat and add vanilla.

Fruit Sauce

Dilute a marmalade or jelly like currant, blueberry, or strawberry (prepared with raw sugar or honey) slowly in a small amount of water over low heat. Add lemon or orange juice.

Sauce Blanche

2 tablespoons unbleached
    wheat flour
1 pint milk

½ cup water
2 ounces butter

Blend the flour and water to make a heavy paste. Bring the milk to a boil and pour the mixture slowly into it. Stir constantly for five minutes. Add salt and butter.

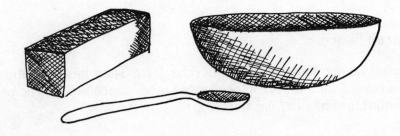

Sauce Béchamel

This sauce was invented, so they say, by an eighteenth century French courtier and financier named Louis de Béchamel.

1 cup milk
1 cup cream
1 ounce butter
½ cup water

2 tablespoons unbleached
    flour
2 tablespoons Parmesan
    cheese, grated

Blend the flour and water to make a heavy paste. Bring the milk to a boil and slowly add mixture to it. Make the same way as the Sauce Blanche. After it has cooked, add the cream slowly, then grated cheese and allow to dissolve in the heat. Add salt and butter stirring gently.

Sour Cream Sauce

Here is a sauce that is quick and easy to make.

1 cup sour cream   *salt*
1 tablespoon milk   *dash of paprika*
1 egg yolk   *juice of one lemon*

Over very low heat, or in a double boiler, heat sour cream with the milk. When the cream is liquid, add the egg yolk, salt and paprika. Stirring constantly add the lemon juice drop by drop.

Nut Flavored Sauce

2 tablespoons peanut or sesame oil
¼ cup of peanut butter (not toasted) or sesame seed butter

2 tablespoons whole wheat flour
1 cup milk
seasonings

Heat the oil in double boiler and blend in the nut or sesame seed butter. Mix the flour into the milk and add it to the oil, stirring until smooth. Cook over boiling water until thick, stirring constantly. Add seasonings. Serve on cooked vegetables.

Sauce Mornay

2 tablespoons butter
2 tablespoons flour
1¾ cup milk, scalded
2 tablespoons Swiss cheese, grated

2 tablespoons Parmesan cheese, grated
2 ounces cream
1 egg yolk
salt
dash of nutmeg

Melt butter in double boiler and blend with flour. Add milk, stirring until creamy and smooth. Add cream and cheese and continue stirring until melted. Beat egg yolk and add a small amount of the hot sauce. Return to double boiler stirring constantly. Add seasonings. Serve hot.

Lemon Butter Sauce

4 ounces butter
1 tablespoon parsley

juice of one lemon
seasonings

Melt butter. Slowly add lemon juice and then parsley. Serve hot over broccoli or other vegetable.

Mustard Sauce

2 tablespoons French
  mustard
1 teaspoon sea salt
1 teaspoon paprika
1 teaspoon brown sugar

olive oil, as much as can
  be absorbed
juice of one lemon
1 teaspoon parsley, chopped

Combine mustard, salt, sugar, paprika, and slowly add oil, drop by drop, stirring continuously until mixture reaches the consistency of mayonnaise. Add lemon juice very slowly, continuing to stir. Add chopped parsley. Allow to infuse for at least one hour.

Sauce Polonaise

4 ounces butter or vegetable
  butter
4 ounces sunflower or
  sesame oil

4 tablespoons bread crumbs
few drops lemon juice

In double boiler melt butter and beat together with oil. Add a few drops of lemon juice and bread crumbs. Serve hot on cauliflower or asparagus.

Sauce Tartare

1 cup fresh Mayonnaise
  (page 28)
1 teaspoon pickle, chopped

1 teaspoon chives, chopped
1 teaspoon capers
1 teaspoon parsley, chopped

Mix all ingredients thoroughly.

Tomato Sauce

1 cup fresh tomato puree or
  6 ounces Italian tomato paste
8 ounces water
1 teaspoon oregano

1 teaspoon sugar
1 tablespoon olive oil
1 teaspoon basil
seasonings

In a saucepan mix tomato and water. Add oil, sugar, herbs and seasonings. Simmer for 30 minutes.

Yogurt Sauce

4 tablespoons natural yogurt
2 tablespoons lemon juice
sea salt

chives, chopped
paprika

Add lemon juice a few drops at a time to the yogurt, stirring constantly. Add seasoning and chives and mix thoroughly. Prepare just before serving. Good on green salads or raw vegetables.

EIGHT

Soups

Soups are often overcooked and frequently contain too much liquid, causing the vegetables to lose much of their nutritional value. Therefore, I prefer to boil my soups as little as possible, and then put them in the blender.

You can also make soups from raw vegetables in a blender. For example:

1 carrot
1 onion
1 stalk celery
few leaves lettuce, romaine,
   or spinach
sea kelp or salt

¼ beet
¼ avocado
1 tablespoon sour cream or
   yogurt
1 pint tomato or
   vegetable juice

Blend all ingredients. Top off with sunflower meal and fresh parsley. How delicious and healthy!

or,

2 tomatoes
1 stalk celery
¼ onion
2 zucchini
fresh basil

½ avocado
1 pint vegetable juice or
   broth
1 tablespoon sour cream or
   heavy yogurt
seasonings

Again, blend all ingredients and garnish with sesame seed meal.

Use your own taste and the vegetables you have available. The important thing is that the ingredients are uncooked.

During periods of fasting, which every health-minded person does at some time, it may be convenient to make a vegetable broth, drinking one cup every hour. Without salt, cook:

2 carrots with tops   *2 stalks celery with leaves*
2 beets with tops   *few leaves of spinach*
1 onion   *half bunch of watercress*
1 leek   *1 tomato (in season)*
parsley   *2 quarts of water*

Cook and discard the vegetables. Use only the broth.

Cold Soups

Minute Borscht

Borscht is a delicious Russian soup, but it normally takes a long time to make. Here is a recipe you can make in minutes by using beets in beet juice available in a jar. Especially good during the hot summer days when you don't feel like cooking.

6 beets   *4 hard-boiled eggs, sliced*
1 medium can vegetable   *¼ cup dill, chives or parsley,*
* juice*   * chopped*
2 cups beet juice   *sour cream*
½ small cucumber, sliced   *2 scallions*
juice of one lemon

From the jar, remove and slice six beets. Mix the vegetable juice, beet juice, cucumbers, scallions, herbs and lemon juice. Chill for ten minutes in the freezer. When ready to serve, add the sliced egg and one spoon of sour cream per plate. Serves three or four.

Tartar Soup

1 large cucumber
1 onion
4 tablespoons sour cream
salt

2 tablespoons instant
   tapioca
2 pints vegetable juice
dill and chives, chopped

Peel and slice cucumber into small pieces. Chop onion and blend together in blender. Move to saucepan and add vegetable juice to the mixture. Sprinkle with tapioca and bring to a boil. Season to taste and chill. Garnish with a slice of cucumber, chopped dill and chives. Serve with dollop of sour cream. Serves four.

Cucumber Yogurt (Yoghourt aux Concombres)

1 pint plain yogurt
1 large cucumber, finely
   chopped
2 scallions, chopped

1 tablespoon fresh mint,
   chopped
salt, paprika to taste

Beat yogurt until smooth. Mix with cucumber and scallions. Season. Top with mint and chill. Eat like a soup. Very cooling on a hot day!

Cold Spinach Soup (Soupe Froide d'Épinards)

2 pounds fresh spinach or
   2 packages frozen
   spinach leaves
2 cups water

1 tablespoon unbleached
   flour
1 cup milk
½ pint heavy cream
1 egg

Wash fresh or thaw frozen spinach. Steam for ten minutes with two cups water. Strain when ready, saving the water. Dissolve the flour in the spinach water and cook until smooth, adding more water if necessary. Then pour into blender with spinach, milk, cream, egg, sugar and seasonings and blend until creamy. Chill and garnish with parsley. Serves four.

The cream can be replaced with sour cream or yogurt.

Vichyssoise

4 large potatoes
1 onion, chopped
1 leek, chopped
1 quart water

1 cup milk
2 ounces butter
¼ cup chives, minced
sour cream
seasonings

Combine in a pot, potatoes, onion, leek and water and boil gently for thirty minutes. Puree the mixture. Add milk, seasonings and butter. Top with spoonful of sour cream and sprinkle with chives. Serves four to six.

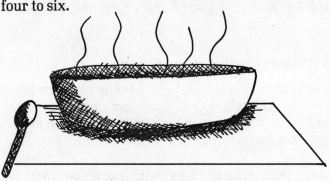

Hot Soups

Minestrone Florentine

1 large red onion, chopped
2 cloves garlic, chopped
3 stalks celery, chopped
2 tablespoons olive oil
4 carrots, sliced
2 quarts boiling water
salt

½ teaspoon oregano
¼ teaspoon basil
1 small can tomato paste
1 cup green peas
4 ounces pastina (tiny egg
   noodles)
grated cheese

Saute onion, garlic, celery in one tablespoon oil for a few minutes. Add the carrots and cook slowly for about seven minutes. Then add water, salt and herbs and let boil for another fifteen minutes. Add the tomato paste, peas, and pastina and cook for an additional fifteen minutes. Before serving, add the other tablespoon of oil and serve with grated cheese. Serves six.

Spanish Soup

2 tablespoons olive oil
3 stalks celery, chopped
1 red onion, chopped
3 shallots, chopped
3 tablespoons tomato puree

1 quart water
1 sprig fresh basil
6 tomatoes, skinned
3 tablespoons instant
   tapioca
1 sprig fresh dill

Heat oil and saute celery, onion, shallots. Add tomatoes, water, salt and basil; cover and simmer for thirty minutes. Add tomato puree and cook again for ten minutes. Puree in blender. Return to pot, and add tapioca and bring back to a boil. Garnish with chopped dill. Serve hot or chilled. Serves six.

French Soup

This is a typical French soup as served at home during the winter months. It is very simple to make.

2 leeks, chopped
4 large potatoes, cubed
1 cup milk
1 ounce butter
seasonings

1 onion, chopped
1 quart water
¼ cup sour cream
¼ cup chives and parsley,
   chopped

Combine water, potatoes, onion and leeks, including greens, in pot. Cover and simmer for thirty-five minutes and serve.

Or if you prefer, puree mixture and return to pot. Add milk, salt and butter and reheat. Add sour cream and garnish with chives and parsley. Serve with croutons. Serves six.

Cream of Asparagus Soup

When you prepare asparagus, save the tops for a tasty soup.

tops of a bunch of asparagus
1 quart water
1 onion
salt

1 tablespoon white flour or
    rice flour
1 cup milk, cold
½ pint cream
1 teaspoon tarragon leaves

Clean asparagus tops and put them in the water with the onion and salt. Cook for forty-five to sixty minutes. Pass through a sieve and return to the cookware. Blend the flour in the milk. Pour the mixture into the warm broth. Cook several minutes, turning slowly. Add a few heads of asparagus, the cream and herbs.

Vegetable Soup

2 carrots
1 beet with the tips
2 potatoes
1 onion
seasonings

1 leek
1 squash
1½ quarts water
½ cup parsley, chopped

Slice vegetables and simmer for forty minutes. Mix in blender, adding seasonings and butter. Top each serving with sunflower meal or nutritional yeast powder. Serves four to six.

Watercress Soup

4 potatoes, diced
1 bunch watercress
1 pint sour cream

1 quart water
1 onion, chopped
salt, pepper

Put potatoes and onion into cold water with the watercress and boil for about thirty minutes. Puree in blender, add cream and serve hot. Serves four to six.

Sorrel Soup

1 bunch of sorrel leaves
1 quart water, lukewarm
1 onion, chopped
2 tablespoons parsley,
    chopped

3 medium potatoes, peeled
    and cubed
1 whole egg
butter and seasoning

Melt sorrel in buttered saucepan. Add water, onion and potatoes and cook until tender. Blend in blender or if not available, mash potatoes. Add the beaten egg and parsley. Serve hot or cold with dollop of sour cream. Serves four.

Onion Soup

2 medium Spanish onions
3 tablespoons safflower oil
1 quart hot water
salt and pepper
2 tablespoons Parmesan
    cheese, grated

4 slices French or
    soya bread, toasted
    and buttered
4 slices Swiss cheese

Brown onions in oiled skillet. Transfer to pot and add hot water and seasonings. Simmer over low heat for twenty-five minutes. Add the Parmesan and transfer into four individual, small *marmites* or earthenware pots. Float the toasted bread in each and top with slices of Swiss cheese. Heat in moderate oven to melt. Serves four.

Onion Soup (Lyonnaise)

2 large onions, chopped
3 tablespoons oil
1 quart hot water
½ cup grated Swiss cheese

1 whole egg, beaten
seasonings
4 slices bread, cubed and
    toasted in butter
    (croutons)

Brown onions in an oiled skillet. Transfer to cooking pot with water and simmer over low heat for thirty minutes. Drain and discard the onions. Mix the broth with grated cheese and egg. Serve with croutons and add more grated cheese.

Peanut Vegetable Soup

1 cup natural chunky peanut butter	2 ounces peanut oil
1 large onion, diced	1 tablespoon flour
2 carrots, diced	½ gallon water or vegetable stock
3 stalks celery, diced	salt
1 large potato, diced	pepper
½ medium-size cabbage, shredded	bay leaf
1 cup fresh tomato, pureed	rosemary
	oregano

In a large kettle, saute all the hard vegetables in peanut oil until glossy, but not soft. Sprinkle flour evenly and mix well. Add water or stock, seasoning to taste. Bring to a boil, stirring constantly. Add peanut butter, tomato puree and shredded cabbage. Mix well and simmer for 15 minutes or until vegetables are cooked to desired doneness.

Created by Tony Santa Elena, Jr., The Good Earth, San Francisco.

Pumpkin Soup

6 cups cut fresh pumpkin, peeled	salt to taste
4 cups water	2 cups milk
1 large onion, sliced	2 tablespoons cornstarch
3 cloves garlic	1 teaspoon brown sugar

Cut pumpkin into cubes and boil in water with onion, garlic, and salt. When tender, put into blender and mix until creamy. Warm again, adding milk, cornstarch, and brown sugar. Cook until ready and serve with butter or cream on top, and croutons. Serves four.

Croutons

To make croutons, cut French or Italian bread into one-half inch cubes. Saute in oil, butter or margarine until light brown.

For garlic croutons, add one or two teaspoons of freshly chopped garlic to cooking oil before sauteing.

Romaine Soup (Soupe de Salade Romaine)

1 small head romaine lettuce
butter or margarine
5 cups warm water
1 onion, sliced

4 potatoes, peeled and
*   cut in cubes*
2 carrots, sliced
salt to taste

Wash and cut lettuce into pieces. Saute with a small amount of butter or margarine (no oil because of the milk). Let cook until the leaves are almost pureed; then add warm water, onions, potatoes, and carrots. Simmer on low heat for thirty minutes. Mix in blender with milk. Heat again and serve with croutons. Serves four.

Lentil Soup (Soupe de Lentilles)

1 cup (8 ounces) lentils
5 cups water
1 onion, sliced
2 shallots, sliced
1 clove garlic

1 carrot
1 stalk celery, cut into pieces
1 bay leaf
salt to taste
1 cup milk

Wash lentils and simmer with other ingredients, except the milk, on low heat about forty-five minutes. When ready, mix thoroughly in blender with milk. Reheat and serve with sour cream and croutons.

Escarole Soup (Soupe d'Escarole)

1 small head escarole
2 tablespoons oil or butter
cups warm water
1 large onion, chopped

4 large potatoes, peeled
*   and cut in small pieces*
sea salt to taste

Wash and chop escarole leaves. Saute with oil or butter. When leaves become dark and soft, add the warm water, onion, and potatoes. Simmer on low heat for about forty to forty-five minutes. Season. Serve with sour cream and toast. Serves four.

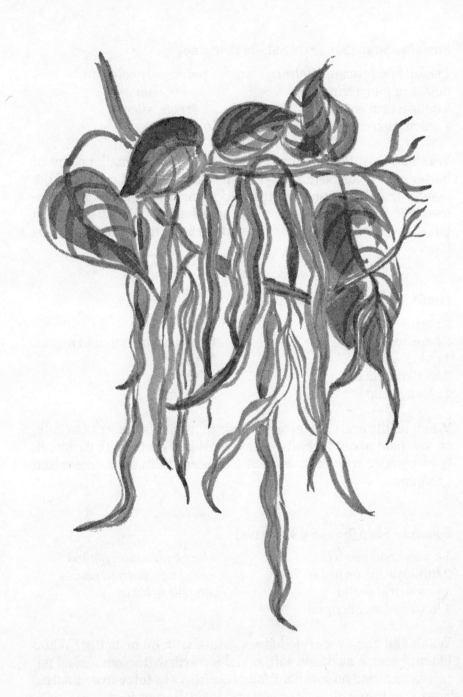

NINE

Vegetables

Artichokes (Artichauts)

Serve one per person. Cut off stem, remove the dried leaves and use kitchen scissors to clip off tips of leaves. Place the artichokes in cold water just to cover the middle of the artichokes. Boil until leaves can be torn off easily. Discard the thistle center. Dip the leaves in sauce. Serve warm with Polonaise Sauce (page 36) or Sour Cream Sauce (page 35), or serve cold with Vinaigrette (page 26).

Artichokes Florentine
A delicious dish.

4 small Italian artichokes	2 tablespoons olive oil
6 ounces tomato paste	1 teaspoon basil
¼ cup garlic, onion, and	1 teaspoon thyme
shallots, chopped	1 teaspoon oregano
8 black olives	dash sugar, seasonings

Remove stem and heavy leaves, leaving only the tender ones. Cut lengthwise into four pieces and discard the thistle center, leaving the heart intact. The heart is the best part. Heat the oil in cookware. Add garlic, shallots and onion, to form a bed for the artichokes to lie on. Add the tomato paste diluted with an equal amount of water. Add herbs, seasonings and sugar if desired. Add water to cover if necessary. Cover tightly and cook for forty-five minutes. If using the small frozen artichokes, twenty-five minutes on very low heat will be sufficient. Add black olives before serving. Serves three or four.

Artichokes Algerian (Artichauts a l'Algérienne)

4 medium artichokes	2 cloves garlic
olive oil	10 black olives, pitted
4 Spanish onions	1 tablespoon parsley, chopped

Wash and remove the tough outer leaves from artichokes. With scissors, clip off about one-half inch from the top of leaves to remove all the prickly points.

Into a heavy skillet, first place two tablespoons of oil, onions, and garlic and saute for a few minutes. Place artichokes on top, cover and simmer on low heat until leaves can be torn off easily. Discard the thistle center and replace by the already cooked onions and garlic. Top with olives and parsley, sprinkle with more oil, and bake in moderate oven for about fifteen minutes. Serve with couscous or rice. Serves four.

Artichokes Barigoule (Artichauts à la Barigoule)

This is a dish from the south of France.

4 onions, chopped	4 cloves garlic, chopped
1 tablespoon olive oil	1 tablespoon finely chopped parsley
2 tablespoons wheat flour	
1 cup water	1 small sprig fresh thyme
4 artichokes	1 small sprig fresh mint
	salt to taste

In a heavy skillet, saute onion in olive oil on low heat for a few minutes. Add flour and water, stirring quickly with a wooden spoon. Place artichokes, cleaned of outer leaves and center and cut into four pieces each, into skillet. Add garlic, parsley, herbs, and salt. If necessary, add more water. Simmer for one hour. Serves four.

Artichokes Provençale (Artichauts à la Provençale)

4 artichokes
5 tomatoes, sliced
olive oil
1 onion, chopped

½ tablespoon thyme
½ tablespoon parsley
juice of one lemon
lemon slices

Wash and cook artichokes in a cup of salted water until leaves tear off easily. Saute tomatoes in olive oil with onion and mushrooms for ten minutes. Add herbs, seasoning and one cup of water. Stir in rice and cook until water is absorbed and rice is tender.

Remove the outer leaves and centers of artichokes. Stuff artichokes with rice and vegetable mixture and sprinkle with lemon juice and parsley.

Arrange on a dish with lettuce leaves, tomato slices, and lemon slices. Can be served hot or cold. Serves four.

Jerusalem Artichokes (Topinambour)
(A tuber, resembling a potato, also called sunchoke.)

One pound per serving. Steam in the skins until easily pierced with a fork. Do not overcook. Remove the skins and place in a saucepan with two tablespoons of oil or butter. Saute for a few minutes. Add lemon juice, salt and paprika.

Asparagus (Asperges)

Prepare one pound per person. Break off each stalk as far down as it breaks easily. Save the discarded part for soup. Tie the stalks together and steam them until tender or about twenty minutes. Serve warm with Lemon Butter Sauce (page 36), Polonaise (page 36), or Sour Cream Sauce (page 35). Serve cold with Vinaigrette (page 26) or Mayonnaise (page 28).

String Beans Mignonnette

2 pounds fresh string beans,
  sliced into strips
3 medium zucchini
1 large onion, sliced
2 tablespoons sunflower
  oil or safflower oil

dash of sea salt
1 teaspoon thyme
½ teaspoon sweet
  marjoram

Oil the bottom of a steel pan or Dutch oven. First add the onion, then the zucchini with the skin on, if not sprayed, then the string beans and herbs. Add ¼ cup of water and cover tightly. Cook on very low heat for about twenty minutes. Serves four.

String Beans Almondine

Proceed as for Mignonnette, but substitute ½ pound of fresh mushrooms for zucchini. Five minutes before done add twelve blanched almonds.

Italian Beans (Fagioletti)

1½ pounds Italian
  green beans
2 tablespoons olive oil
1 red onion, sliced
1 small can tomato paste

¼ cup water
2 cloves garlic
½ teaspoon oregano
½ teaspoon basil

Oil pan and add onion, garlic and beans. Dissolve the tomato paste in water and add seasonings herbs, and a dash of raw sugar. Pour over the beans and cook for 15 minutes.

Soy Beans

Soak dried soy beans overnight. Then simmer in the same water on low heat with a minimum of stirring, for two to three hours. For each cup of dried soy beans use three cups of water.

Stewed Soy Beans

1 cup soy beans, cooked
1 onion, chopped
2 stalks celery, chopped
2 tomatoes
soy oil as desired

1 bay leaf
1 tablespoon molasses
½ cup of water with
   1 tablespoon cider vinegar
1 teaspoon sage

Saute onion, celery and tomatoes in oil. Add water, soy beans, bay leaf and molasses and stew for about fifteen minutes. When ready, season and add soy oil. Serves three or four.

Wax Beans

2 pounds wax beans
3 tablespoons olive oil
4 fresh tomatoes

¼ cup garlic, chopped
shallots and onions

Pour two tablespoons of oil into steel cookware and saute garlic, onions, and shallots for five minutes. Add beans cut in one inch lengths. Place tomatoes on top and add one ounce of water. Cover tightly and cook until tender adding more water if necessary. Add salt and the remaining oil. Serve with fresh chopped basil and parsley.

Italian Beans (Fresh White Bush Beans)

The country people of Tuscany prepare fresh beans in this delicious way. For the best flavor use earthenware as they do. However, a Dutch oven or other casserole may be used.

4 pounds fresh bush beans
   in pods
4 cloves garlic
1 large onion
1 sprig fresh basil
few rosemary leaves

4 fresh tomatoes
4 shallots
¼ cup olive oil
1 sprig fresh thyme
1 tablespoon brown sugar
salt to taste

Chop garlic, shallots and onion and combine with other ingredients. Fill casserole with water to cover the beans. Add the herbs and one tablespoon of brown sugar. Bake covered for two hours at 350°.

Lima Beans (Feves)

Lima beans mix well with other vegetables. To serve separately, allow about one pound of fresh beans per person. Heat one tablespoon of oil in cookware and add chopped garlic, lima beans, and enough water to cover. When tender, water should be evaporated. Season with butter, salt, paprika and chopped parsley.

Beets (Betteraves)

Beets can be used either raw or cooked in a salad or in soup and vegetable dishes. The tops, if crisp and fresh, can be used in salads or cooked in soups also. Steam whole beets until tender. Remove skin, slice and season with butter and lemon juice, or serve cold in a green salad.

Broccoli

Broccoli should look green and fresh. Wash carefully and stew with other vegetables or steam until tender. Serve with Polonaise Sauce (page 36) or Lemon Butter Sauce (page 36). Cold, they also make a good salad.

Brussels Sprouts (Choux de Bruxelles)

Brussels sprouts should be crisp and green. Remove loose leaves and wash carefully as they often contain insects. Steam or cook in a small amount of water until tender. Serve with oil or butter and grated cheese. Prepare one-half pound per serving.

Red Cabbage (Chou Rouge)

Serve raw, shredded, mixed with salads or stewed with other vegetables. To cook it separately, boil the sliced cabbage in a cup of water to which you add the juice of one lemon or one table-spoon of apple cider vinegar. When tender, the water should be evaporated. For a tasty variation, cook it with two peeled and sliced apples. Season with sea salt, oil or butter.

White Cabbage (Chou Blanc)

Cook the same as the red cabbage. Also serve raw, shredded. (see Coleslaw, page 17.)

Candied Onions (Entrée aux Petits Oignons)

1 pound small white onions
of even size
4 tablespoons peanut oil

6 ounces raisins,
soaked in water for
two hours

Peel onions, leaving them whole. Place in pan with oil and simmer on low heat for about fifteen to twenty minutes. Add raisins and salt. Cover and simmer again until the onions look candied. Serves four.

Andalusian Carrots (Carottes à l'Andalouse)

6 ounces raisins
12 carrots

4 ounces butter or
margarine

Soak raisins in warm water for two to three hours. Clean carrots, cut in thin slices and place in a pan with enough water to cover. Simmer, tightly covered, on low heat for thirty minutes until water is absorbed. Pour the raisins with the water and butter over them and simmer about ten more minutes. Serves four.

Minted Carrots (Carottes à la Menthe)

12 young carrots
salt to taste
2 tablespoons raw sugar

4 ounces sweet butter
¼ cup freshly chopped mint

Peel and slice carrots. Place them in a pan with enough water to cover and simmer on medium heat until water is absorbed. Add salt, sugar, butter, and mint. Cover and allow to simmer for a few more minutes. Serves four.

Savoy Cabbage (Chou de Savoie)

1 head Savoy cabbage	1 cup water
2 tablespoons oil	2 bay leaves
2 large onions, chopped	½ teaspoon thyme
2 cloves garlic	½ teaspoon sage
3 large carrots, sliced	4 whole cloves
2 potatoes, sliced	salt and pepper

Cut cabbage in four to six pieces according to size. Pour the oil into a deep pot or Dutch oven. First add onions and garlic, then half of cabbage together with the carrots and potatoes. Place the rest of the cabbage on top and add water, herbs and seasonings. Should not burn if covered tightly and cooked over very low heat for about thirty minutes. Serves three or four.

Carrots (Carottes)

Carrots are roots and contain sugar. I use them in almost every dish, salad and soup, or they can be eaten raw or with dips. Steam them with the skins if they have not been sprayed. Otherwise, peel and wash the carrots before steaming. When tender, remove the skin and serve with fresh butter.

Glazed Carrots

After steaming, slice carrots and place them in a casserole. Add butter and brown sugar or honey and bake until glazed in moderate oven 375°.

Carrots Vichy

Steam and slice carrots. Pour a Sauce Blanche (page 34), over them and add chopped chervil and parsley.

Cauliflower (Chou-Fleur)

Head should be compact with white flowerets. After washing, remove green parts. To eat raw, separate flowerets and dip them in Mayonnaise (page 28), or other dips.

Cauliflower Meranese

Steam the whole head till tender but do not overcook. When cold, arrange on a plate and pour a Mustard Sauce (page 36) with ¼ cup of capers over it. Garnish with cooked, sliced beets around the plate.

Multicolor Cauliflower (Chou-Fleur Multicouleur)

1 large cauliflower	seasonings
½ cup flour	2 tomatoes, sliced
¼ cup water	1 lemon, sliced
1 egg	2 tablespoons parsley, chopped

Wash cauliflower, cut into flowerets and steam in double boiler. Make a light batter of flour, water, egg, one tablespoon oil, and season to taste. Dip flowerets in batter and fry in oil.

Place in serving dish, decorating with slices of tomato and lemon. Top with parsley. Serves four.

Cauliflower à la Blanche

Steam cauliflower but serve warm with a Sauce Blanche (page 34).

Cauliflower au Gratin

Cook cauliflower. Separate the flowerets and put them in an oiled casserole. pour a Sauce Blanche (page 34) over it and top with grated cheese. Bake at 375° until a brown crust forms on top.

Celery (Celeri)

Like carrots, celery is used in salads, soups and vegetable dishes. The best way is to eat it raw. After washing, remove the leaves and cut the stalk into four or five pieces. Fill the scooped portions with anything you like from peanut butter to cheese or a spread.

Celery à la Béchamel

Steam the stalks but don't cook completely. Place them in a casserole and pour a Sauce Bechamel (page 34), over them. Sprinkle
with grated cheese and bake in moderate oven (375°) for about
thirty-five minutes.

Corn (Mais)

Serve one or two ears per person. Remove husks and silks. Steam
or boil in small amount of water for five to ten minutes. Serve on
cob or scrape the kernels off. Delicious when reheated in butter
or Sour Cream Sauce (page 35). Young, tender, fresh and white
corn can be eaten raw.

Grilled Corn

For a picnic, this is a delicious way to prepare corn. Open husks
without removing them, but remove silk. Close husks and wet
thoroughly. Place the cobs on top of the charcoal grill. Serve with
butter.

Cucumbers (Concombres)

Cucumbers are usually eaten raw in salads. They should have a
green lustrous skin. When older they get yellowish. When you
buy them in supermarkets, beware of the heavy waxy finish
often found on them. You can also cook cucumbers like other
vegetables and make cold soups with them.

Eggplant (Aubergine)

There are many tasty recipes for this vegetable, peeled or unpeeled. Do not, however, soak it in water. Eggplant requires a lot
of oil for cooking. Buy a medium size eggplant for two servings.

Stuffed Eggplant Creole

1 medium eggplant
   cut in half
1 large onion, minced
1 stalk celery, diced
½ pound mushrooms, sliced
¼ cup olive oil

⅓ cup bread crumbs
1 teaspoon thyme
1 teaspoon oregano
1 teaspoon basil
sea salt
paprika

Scoop out the pulp leaving the shell ¼ inch thick. Saute the onion in oil, add celery, mushrooms, and chopped pulp of eggplant and cook until eggplant is tender. Add bread crumbs, herbs and spices, mixing well with fork. Fill the eggplant shells with the mixture. Bake in oven at 350° for thirty minutes. Serves two.

Eggplant Martinique

2 medium onions, chopped
2 cloves garlic
2 stalks celery, diced
1 green pepper, chopped
1 teaspoon marjoram
1 teaspoon thyme

1 medium unpeeled eggplant,
   diced
2 tomatoes cut in chunks
¼ cup olive oil
salt
paprika

In a skillet, saute onions, garlic, celery and pepper for five minutes. Add remaining ingredients and mix well. Cover and cook for twenty minutes. Serves two to four.

Eggplant Cutlet

1 medium eggplant
1 egg, beaten
½ cup bread crumbs
oil, enough to fry

1 teaspoon oregano
1 teaspoon garlic powder
grated cheese
salt

Mix bread crumbs with garlic, oregano and salt. Without peeling eggplant, cut it lengthwise into one inch slices. Dip each slice in egg, then in crumbs. Saute in oiled skillet, turning to brown each side. Top with grated cheese. Serves four.

If you do not use eggs, substitute ½ cup of buttermilk. Top with sesame seed meal instead of grated cheese.

Eggplant Athenian (Aubergine à l'Athenienne)

4 medium eggplants
   (one per serving)
2 tomatoes, chopped
4 onions, chopped
4 cloves garlic, chopped
1 teaspoon parsley, chopped
1 teaspoon chervil

1 teaspoon oregano
¼ teaspoon nutmeg
salt and pepper to taste
olive oil
1 tablespoon tomato paste
juice of one lemon

Cut eggplants into four pieces lengthwise, but not completely through at top; scoop out pulp, leaving shell ¼ inch thick.

Mix chopped vegetables with the chopped pulp, add herbs and seasonings. Stir well and stuff mixture into eggplant shells, tying shut with string. Place into heavy skillet with four tablespoons oil on a bed of chopped onions. Add tomato paste combined with small amount of water, and lemon juice. Cover tightly and simmer on low heat for one hour. Serve hot with brown rice. Serves four.

Eggplant Genovese

1 large eggplant
1 mozzarella cheese, sliced
12 ounces tomato paste
2 tablespoons olive oil

1 teaspoon salt
1 teaspoon brown sugar
1 teaspoon oregano
1 teaspoon basil
dash garlic powder

Mix the tomato paste with an equal amount of water. Add herbs, salt and sugar and simmer on low heat to a boil.

Cut the eggplant in one inch slices, lengthwise. Pour oil in casserole and alternate layers of eggplant slices with cheese, finishing with the cheese. Pour the tomato sauce over it and bake in preheated oven at 375°for thirty-five to forty minutes. Serves six.

Endive

Allied to chicory, endive is bitter to the taste and is generally used in salads, but you can also prepare a tasty dish with them.

Broiled Endive (Endive Braisée)

Endive becomes bitter on contact with water. Therefore, wash rapidly without opening the leaves and dry on absorbent towel. Steam until tender. Place in an oiled broiling dish, adding salt and dotting with butter. Broil until slightly brown. Sprinkle with lemon juice or serve with grated cheese.

Fennel (Fenouil)

Fennel has a delicate aroma similar to anise. One medium fennel is enough for two to three persons. After removing the outer leaves, cut the fennel lengthwise into four pieces. Steam until tender. Serve with Sour Cream Sauce (page 35). Fennel may be baked also, and served with a Béchamel Sauce (page 34).

Kohlrabi (Chou-Rave)

Be sure it has young leaves and roots and is not too large. The small ones taste better and can be eaten raw or chopped into salads. Otherwise, cut into slices, cover with a small amount of water and cook until tender. Season with butter and salt or serve with a White Sauce.

Kale (Chou Frisé)

Kale should look fresh and green. It is rich in minerals but has a strong taste. Wash several times and cook it in water. Prepare approximately one pound per person and serve like spinach.

Leeks (Poireaux)

Leeks are used principally for soups, but cooked like asparagus are also a delicious dish. Remove the outer skin and wash thoroughly because dust often settles between the leaves. Cut off and discard the top half of the green. Steam or boil the leeks in a small amount of water. Serve warm with Lemon Butter Sauce (page 36) or Sour Cream Sauce (page 35), or serve cold with Vinaigrette (page 26).

Lentils (Lentilles)

Lentils contain protein and minerals. They are eaten principally during the winter months, since they are too rich in summer time. They make excellent soups, salads, casseroles and may also be sprouted. Some health food stores have pink lentils, which are very tasty. Wash and clean carefully. For each cup of lentils use three cups of water. Add one onion, two shallots, one carrot and two tablespoons of olive or peanut oil. Simmer slowly for thirty-five minutes, adding more water if necessary. (Please note: the pink ones cook faster.) Serves four.

Mushrooms (Champignons)

There are many species of mushrooms. Since some are very poisonous, buy the cultivated ones. They should be firm, moist, and white. Peel only if they show signs of drying. Wash them thoroughly in cold water to which you have added one tablespoon of cider vinegar. Mushrooms may be eaten raw in a salad or they complement many dishes.

Mushrooms à la Crème

1 pound mushrooms
¼ cup parsley, chopped
2 tablespoons oil or butter

3 tablespoons sour cream
salt and pepper
paprika

Leave mushrooms whole or cut into slices. Cook in oil or butter for ten minutes. When tender, mix the sour cream into the juice of the mushrooms and stir well. Combine with the mushrooms salt, pepper, paprika and parsley. Serves three.

Mushrooms Provençale

1 pound mushrooms, caps
and stems, sliced
3 tablespoons olive oil

¼ cup parsley, chopped
very fine
4 cloves garlic, chopped

Saute garlic in oil over low heat; then add mushrooms and parsley. Season, turning frequently for ten minutes. Serves three.

Grilled Mushrooms

Use large mushroom caps. Brush with oil and place cap side down with a bit of butter in center, season, sprinkle with chopped parsley or chervil. Broil until light brown, approximately six to eight minutes.

Okra

Wash thoroughly and cut off stems. Cook by steaming until tender. Season with butter and salt. Prepare one pound for four servings.

Olives

Black olives add flavor and nourishment to many vegetable dishes. Italian or Greek olives are preferable.

Onions (Oignons)

Onions add flavor to many dishes, salads, soups and entrees. Scallions and chives are of the same family. Red or Spanish onions used raw are the most flavorful.

You can make a delicious dish with small white onions. Peel under water leaving the onions whole. Cook in small amount of water for fifteen minutes. Drain and add a Cream Sauce.

Potatoes (Pommes de Terre)

The best way to retain most of the food value of the potato is by baking. Select potatoes of similar size. Set oven at 350° and allow one hour baking time for large potatoes. Many enjoy the skin as well.

Boiled Potatoes (en Robe de Chambre)

New potatoes are delicious when boiled in their jackets. Cook them in a small amount of water and salt until tender and the water is absorbed. Serve with fresh butter and eat the skin as well.

Variation: When potatoes are cooked, remove skins and pour fresh butter or oil over them. Sprinkle with paprika and chopped parsley or chervil.

Potato Croquettes

You can make leftover mashed potatoes into croquettes. Put the cold mashed potatoes into a bowl and add one or two egg yolks. If you don't eat eggs use grated cheese instead. Add salt and form into little balls. Roll in bread crumbs and bake on oiled sheet until light brown. Serve the croquettes with creamed mushrooms or spinach.

Potatoes Bonne Femme

2 pounds potatoes   salt
¼ cup sunflower oil   chives, chopped
1 pound onions   paprika

Steam or boil potatoes in their skins. Do not overcook. Drain and cool, then peel and slice. Pour some oil into a skillet and fry onions until golden brown. Add potatoes and more oil if necessary, turning constantly until they are crisp and brown. Season and top with chives. Serves four.

Hans' Potato Pancakes

2 cups potatoes
2 eggs, well beaten
salt, pepper or paprika

1 cup bread crumbs
1 small onion

Grate potatoes and onion very fine. Potatoes may be grated in a vegetable mill or a blender but a hand grater gives better results. Add the eggs and bread crumbs, mixing well. Add salt to taste. Pour one tablespoon of the mixture into hot oiled fry pan. Serves four to six.

Sweet Potatoes or Yams

Bake sweet potatoes or yams in their skins to retain the most food value.

Glazed Sweet Potatoes

4 sweet potatoes
¼ cup oil or butter
pinch of cinnamon

juice of one orange
¼ cup raw sugar or
    honey

Steam in their jackets until tender. Peel and cut in half or slice and place in a baking dish. Mix remaining ingredients and pour mixture over potatoes. Bake in moderate oven 350° to 375° until glazed.

Sweet Potato Croquettes

4 sweet potatoes
1 cup bread crumbs
oil, enough to fry

1 egg
1 tablespoon raw sugar
salt

Steam or boil sweet potatoes in their jackets until tender. Peel, mash, add the yolk of the egg, salt, sugar, and half of the bread crumbs. Beat the white of the egg until stiff and stir into mixture. Form croquettes, roll them in bread crumbs and fry slowly in oil, turning carefully to brown each side. Makes six croquettes.

Peas

Fresh, tender, young peas may be served raw or mixed in salads.

French Peas (Petit Pois à la Française)

3 pounds fresh shelled peas
½ head Boston lettuce
6 small white onions
2 teaspoons sugar

2 ounces butter
2 tablespoons oil
salt

Shell peas just before cooking but don't wash them. Pour oil in cookware and add the onions, then half of the lettuce leaves. Place the peas on top and cover with the remaining leaves of lettuce. Add sugar and cook covered on very low heat for about twenty-five minutes. No water is necessary. Season with salt and butter. Serves three.

Stuffed Baked Potato Florentine

4 large russet potatoes,
   unpeeled, scrubbed and
   baked
1 pound fresh spinach,
   chopped
1 medium onion, minced
½ pound fresh mushrooms,
   minced
¼ cup sour cream

3 ounces cheddar cheese,
   shredded
3 ounces jack cheese,
   shredded
salt
white pepper
nutmeg
savory

Cut potatoes in half lengthwise. Hollow out centers to form cup. Mash potatoes and mix well with other ingredients, seasoning to taste. Stuff potato cups with mixture and bake in a preheated oven (375°) for 20 minutes. Serve with a teaspoon of white sauce on top (optional). Serves four.

Created by Tony Santa Elena, Jr., The Good Earth, San Francisco.

Bell Peppers (Poivrons)

Green or red sweet bell peppers may be used. Wash, remove stems and seeds. Leave whole to stuff and bake or chop to serve raw in salads or stew with other vegetables.

Stuffed Green Peppers

6 green peppers
½ cup rice
2 onions, chopped
½ cup grated Parmesan
   cheese

½ teaspoon thyme
½ teaspoon sage
1 teaspoon oregano
1 teaspoon nutritional yeast

Cook rice. Add onions and mix with herbs and cheese. Add rice and yeast. Cut stems from peppers and make a hole in top of pepper to remove seeds. Steam or boil until they turn a dull green. Fill peppers with mixture and place filled peppers on an oiled baking pan. Bake for about twenty-five to thirty minutes in a 350° oven. Serves six.

Red Peppers

You can make preserves of sweet red peppers in the fall. After washing, remove seeds and cut into quarters. Place them skin side up in a baking dish and broil until toasted. Peel as soon as the skin comes off easily. Cut into slices lengthwise and put into a jar. Fill with olive oil, a dash of salt and a sprig of fresh basil. Keep refrigerated. Easy to use any time you like.

Pumpkin and Acorn Squash

Cut into serving pieces and remove seeds. Acorn squash may be cut in half. Place pieces upside down in baking pan with small amount of water. Bake at 400° until tender. Turn over and place a bit of butter or oil on each. Season with salt, paprika, or nutmeg and return to oven for few minutes. Serve in shell.

Spinach (Épinards)

Spinach should be green and crisp; buy one pound for two servings. Wash several times. Spinach makes a delicious salad when eaten raw. To cook, place in pan with a very small amount of water. Don't overcook. Do not drain since spinach contains many minerals and vitamins which are water soluble.

Creamed Spinach

When cooked, chop spinach and season to taste. Add one tablespoon of sour cream per serving and a few drops of honey.

Spinach Meridional

Cook whole spinach leaves. Fry rapidly in olive oil with chopped garlic.

Spinach Soufflé

2 pounds fresh spinach
2 tablespoons unbleached
    flour
2 eggs, separated

2 tablespoons butter
1 cup milk
salt, dash of sugar

Cook and chop spinach or blend in blender. Make a sauce with milk, flour and butter. Combine egg yolks, sauce and spinach. Fold in stiffly beaten egg whites. Pour into an oiled casserole and sprinkle with grated cheese. Bake at 350° about thirty minutes. Serves four.

Swiss Chard

When very fresh, chard may be used in salad. To cook, prepare and serve like spinach.

Sorrel (Oseille)

Sorrel is a fleshy, acid-leaved green. When young and fresh it may be used in salads. Or cook and mix with spinach. Also makes a tasty soup (page 45).

Turnips

Turnips are an edible root, allied to rutabaga. They should have crisp, green tops. Peel carefully and slice. Steam or boil in small amount of water until tender. Season with salt and butter or oil.

Variation: Cook the turnips with carrots and mash. Add milk, butter and seasonings.

Tomatoes (Tomates)

Tomatoes have many uses, from soups to sauces, and complement almost every dish. To serve raw, I like tomatoes bright red in color and ripe. Some prefer them firm and not so ripe. The yellow tomato contains less acid. For people with delicate stomachs it is preferable to peel tomatoes. The easy way is to plunge them in and out of boiling water. Skin will come off easily.

Broiled Tomatoes

Slice tomatoes and roll in bread crumbs. Place under broiler for about ten minutes until browned.

Tomatoes Provençale (Tomates Provençales)

1 or 2 tomatoes per serving	olive oil
1 teaspoon chopped parsley per tomato	paprika
1 clove garlic per tomato	salt

Cut tomatoes in half and arrange cut side down in oiled skillet and cook at moderate heat for three minutes. Turn over and place chopped garlic and parsley on top. Season, cover and lower the heat. Cook for about fifteen minutes. Remove cover and let the juice be absorbed. Delicious on top of an omelette or with a fresh ear of corn.

Grandma's Stuffed Tomatoes

6 large tomatoes	2 slices corn bread
1 small onion, minced	½ cup milk, or, if you prefer,
¼ cup bread crumbs	vegetable juice
1 clove garlic, chopped	1 teaspoon basil
salt to taste	1 teaspoon oregano

Wash and cut a thin slice from stem end of tomatoes. Scoop out and save the pulp. Saute onion and garlic in oil until golden. Soak the slices of bread in milk or juice. Add the chopped, drained pulp, herbs, onion, garlic, seasonings and bread crumbs. Fill tomatoes with the mixture and sprinkle top with cheese. Place in oiled, shallow baking dish. Bake about thirty minutes at 350°. Serves six.

Tomato Puree for Sauce

10 tomatoes, peeled	1 teaspoon basil
3 cloves garlic, chopped	3 onions, chopped
3 tablespoons olive oil	1 teaspoon oregano
salt and pepper to taste	

Wash, peel and stew tomatoes for ten minutes. Put through food mill or blend in blender. Saute onions and garlic in oil for about five minutes. Add the tomato puree, herbs, seasonings, and simmer for a long time to desired consistency.

Zucchini (Courgettes)

The raw, tender, young zucchini may be grated or cut into thin slices for salads. It can also be cooked and mixed with other vegetables.

Broiled Zucchini

Cut zucchini into thin slices with the skin on. Place in oiled pan and sprinkle with oil, grated cheese, and seasonings. Broil for about ten minutes.

Zucchini à la Béchamel

Steam whole zucchini with skin on for fifteen minutes. Slice lengthwise and cover with Béchamel Sauce (page 34). Sprinkle with grated cheese and bake in 350° oven for thirty-five minutes.

Stuffed Zucchini à la Bordelaise

4 zucchini
3 slices soy or corn bread
½ cup tomato juice or broth
½ cup bread crumbs
4 cloves garlic, chopped
salt, paprika

1 teaspoon marjoram
1 teaspoon oregano
1 teaspoon basil
1 small onion, chopped
1 tablespoon olive oil

Steam whole zucchini in skin for fifteen minutes. Cut zucchini lengthwise and scoop out centers saving pulp. Soak slices of bread in juice or broth. Mash and add crushed zucchini pulp, herbs, half of the bread crumbs, seasoning, oil, garlic and onions, mixing well. Stuff zucchini shells with the mixture. Sprinkle with paprika and the rest of the bread crumbs. Bake in oiled pan for forty-five minutes at 350°. Serves four.

Zucchini Fritters (Beignets de Courgettes)

½ cup flour
½ cup water
salt to taste
2 egg yolks

2 egg whites, beaten
2 medium zucchini
parsley and lemon
  slices to garnish

Make a batter with flour, water, salt, and egg yolks. Fold in beaten egg whites. Cut zucchini in ¼-inch slices and sprinkle with additional flour. Dip each slice into batter and fry in oil over medium heat. Serve immediately with parsley and lemon. Serves four.

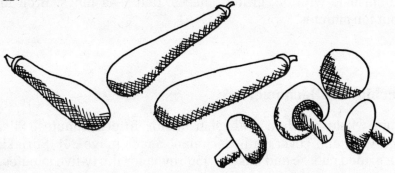

Zucchini Casserole (Plat de Courgettes)

4 medium zucchini
½ pound mushrooms
½ pint sour cream
1 tablespoon fresh dill,
  chopped

1 tablespoon parsley,
  chopped
2 tablespoons Parmesan
  cheese, grated
1 tablespoon unbleached
  flour

Wash zucchini, leaving skins on. Cut into pieces and steam in small amount of water. Wash and cut mushrooms in half and cook over medium heat in buttered skillet. Blend flour with water left from zucchini, add to mushrooms and cook for a few minutes; add sour cream, seasoning, herbs and mix well.

Place zucchini in buttered casserole, add mixture, and top with cheese; broil for ten to fifteen minutes. Serves four.

Stuffed Zucchini au Gratin

4 zucchini, short and thick
½ cup whole grain brown
   rice, cooked
¼ cup wheat berries,
   cooked
2 ounces onions, finely chopped
2 ounces celery, finely chopped
4 ounces fresh tomatoes, pureed
2 ounces Parmesan cheese
2 ounces ricotta cheese

2 ounces cheddar cheese,
   shredded
2 ounces bread crumbs
2 ounces oil
salt
ground black pepper
oregano
thyme
garlic powder

Cut zucchini in half lengthwise. Hollow out centers to form cup. Chop zucchini meat and mix well with other ingredients, seasoning to taste. Stuff zucchini cups with mixture. Wrap individually in foil and bake in preheated oven for twenty-five minutes. Serve with basic tomato sauce on top (optional).

Created by Tony Santa Elena, Jr., The Good Earth, San Francisco.

TEN

Mixed Vegetables

Cook vegetables together. First cook the ones which contain more juice such as onions, greens, zucchini and tomatoes. They can be cooked without adding water. Others absorb the juice such as potatoes, carrots and turnips. Always mix the two kinds so you need not add water. In this way the vegetables retain all their natural flavor and nutritional value. Be sure you have a tight fitting lid to prevent the loss of steam.

Potée Normande

2 pounds Savoy cabbage, finely cut	1 large onion, chopped
	¼ teaspoon nutmeg
4 carrots, sliced	½ teaspoon thyme
4 potatoes, sliced	1 bay leaf
2 tablespoons oil	salt, paprika

In a Dutch oven or steel cookware, pour two tablespoons of your favorite oil. Then add onions, half of the cabbage, the carrots and potatoes and finish with the remaining cabbage. Add herbs and cover tightly. Cook thirty minutes and salt to taste. Serves four.

Ratatouille Niçoise

¼ cup olive oil
1 green pepper, chopped
1 large onion, chopped
3 cloves garlic, chopped
3 zucchini, sliced
4 tomatoes, sliced

1 eggplant, sliced
½ teaspoon oregano
½ teaspoon basil
½ teaspoon thyme
2 tablespoons tomato paste
salt, pepper

Saute in oil onion, garlic, and green pepper for a few minutes. First add a layer of zucchini, then two tomatoes sliced, a layer of eggplant and finish with the remaining tomatoes and herbs. Cover tightly and cook at very low heat for forty-five minutes. Add tomato paste and season to taste, adding oil if necessary. Cook ten minutes more. Serve warm with rice or noodles or chilled with the juice of one lemon. Serves four.

Vegetables with Aioli (Aioli Niçois)

Aioli is a typical southern French sauce served with fish or meat. Here is a vegetarian version.

4 potatoes
4 small zucchini, sliced
2 tomatoes, sliced

½ pound Italian string
  beans
1 onion chopped
1 stalk celery

Steam potatoes in their skins. Simmer other vegetables together with a small amount of oil on low heat.

For the aioli sauce:

6 cloves garlic
1 egg yolk
1 teaspoon mustard
1 teaspoon honey

olive oil
lemon juice or vinegar
salt, pepper or paprika

Crush garlic to form a paste. In a bowl, beat egg yolk with mustard, honey and seasonings. Add oil slowly, drop by drop, beating with a fork. Add garlic, continuing to beat. Sauce should acquire consistency of mayonnaise. Add lemon juice, drop by drop, and parsley.

Peel and slice potatoes, placing them around the vegetables arranged in a dish. Serve with aioli. Serves four.

Vegetables Primavera

Take the first spring vegetables from your own garden, or from a farm stand, and prepare this delicious dish.

1 cup young peas, shelled
1 cup fresh string beans,
    diced
2 zucchini, sliced
3 new potatoes, diced
few leaves of Boston lettuce
1 bay leaf

4 onions, chopped
6 young carrots, sliced
¼ cup water
1 tablespoon oil
1 sprig of parsley
1 sprig chervil
seasonings

Oil the bottom of the cookware. Add the onions and place the leaves of the lettuces on top. Add peas, beans, carrots, potatoes, zucchini with the skin on and finally the herbs. Add water if necessary, cover tightly and cook on low heat for twenty-five minutes. Season to taste. Serves six.

Potée Brumaire

2 onions, chopped
1 turnip, diced
1 beet, diced
2 carrots, diced
1 tablespoon sesame oil

2 celery stalks, chopped
1 small winter squash
few leaves Swiss chard
1 teaspoon thyme
1 bay leaf
¼ teaspoon caraway seeds

Layer ingredients in oiled baking dish, starting with onions, celery, chard and finishing with squash. Add herbs and cook at low heat for forty-five minutes. Serves four.

Corn with Rosemary

1 onion, chopped	6 ounces fresh peas
1 green pepper, chopped	2 tablespoons corn oil
6 ounces corn	¼ cup water
1 zucchini, diced	½ teaspoon thyme
seasoning	½ teaspoon rosemary

Saute onion and green pepper in oil for a few minutes. Add corn, peas and zucchini. Cover, add water if necessary and simmer twenty-five minutes. Serves three.

Winter Mixture

1 pound fresh Brussels sprouts	1 onion, minced
1 small eggplant, diced	1 clove garlic
1 large carrot, diced	½ teaspoon marjoram
½ pound mushrooms	½ teaspoon sage

In oiled cookware, place onion, garlic, eggplant, mushrooms, carrots and sprouts. Add one tablespoon of water if necessary and simmer for thirty minutes. Serves four.

Vegetarian Gratiné

1 cup macaroni	¼ cup grated cheddar cheese
2 quarts boiling water, salted	2 ounces butter
2 cups mixed vegetables, such as celery, carrots, peppers, onions, mushrooms	1 cup milk
	¼ cup whole wheat bread crumbs

If possible use macaroni which are made of Jerusalem artichokes or spinach. Cook it in salted boiling water about twenty minutes or until tender. Rinse with cold water, let stand for a few minutes and drain. Cook vegetables until tender and combine with macaroni. Mix the milk, butter and cheese. Season to taste and pour over macaroni and vegetables. Place in oiled casserole and sprinkle with more cheese. Cover with bread crumbs and bake in oven 350° oven for about thirty minutes. Serves six.

Vegetarian Stew Meridional

1 medium eggplant, peeled
2 large carrots, diced
10 mushrooms, sliced
2 cups tomato juice
¼ teaspoon oregano

¼ teaspoon marjoram
2 cloves garlic
2 tablespoons tomato paste
3 tablespoons olive or
    peanut oil

Saute garlic and eggplant in oil for few minutes. Add carrots and juice and let simmer for fifteen minutes. Add mushrooms, herbs and tomato paste and let simmer for fifteen minutes more. Season to taste, serve with rice or pasta. Serves four.

Summer Jardinière

1 pound young onions,
    minced
1 pound tomatoes, sliced
1 cup fresh peas or
    lima beans
½ pound mushrooms

1 pound zucchini, sliced
1 small eggplant, sliced
1 clove garlic
3 tablespoons oil
parsley, chervil, chives,
    seasoning

Place ingredients into oiled cookware and simmer for twenty minutes. Season and add more oil if necessary. Serves six.

Pipérade

8 ripe tomatoes, peeled
    and sliced
2 green peppers, cleaned,
    chopped

¼ pound couscous
2 cloves garlic
2 tablespoons olive oil

In oiled Dutch oven cook tomatoes, peppers and garlic for twenty-five minutes. Wet couscous with a glass of warm water and pour over vegetables. Mix well, cover and let cook thirty minutes longer on very low heat. Add seasoning and butter. Serve hot. Serves four.

Sauerkraut (Choucroute Vegetarienne)

2 pounds sauerkraut   4 apples
8 sausages, meatless   juice of one lemon
4 potatoes, peeled and boiled

Wash sauerkraut, peel and slice apples, place both in oiled Dutch oven and cook for one hour or more on very low heat. Add the lemon juice and seasonings and serve with potatoes and sausage substitute. Season. Serves four.

Philippine Chop Suey

4 carrots, thinly sliced   ½ pound pea pods,
½ pound long string beans,   fresh or frozen
   cut into pieces   few leaves Chinese cabbage
1 large onion, chopped   1 pound Oriental noodles
1 green pepper, chopped   (made with rice flour)

Saute the vegetables in a heavy skillet in small amount of soy oil, turning constantly with a wooden spoon until slightly cooked. Remove from heat. Bring two pints of water or broth to a boil in a saucepan and cook noodles, stirring constantly, until tender. Drain noodles and combine with vegetables. Season to taste and continue to cook for a few minutes, turning constantly. Serves four.

ELEVEN

Rice

Use natural brown rice instead of polished white rice. It takes longer to cook but brown rice contains all the nutrients. Wash rice carefully and use three cups of water for each cup of rice. Add some herbs such as sage, thyme, marjoram and a bay leaf. Salt and cover. Allow to simmer gently for forty to forty-five minutes until the water is completely absorbed.

Risotto

1 cup raw brown rice
2 tablespoons olive oil
1 onion, chopped
1 clove garlic, chopped
2 cups hot water

½ teaspoon saffron
½ teaspoon oregano
½ teaspoon powdered
  rosemary
1 cup tomato sauce
½ cup grated cheese

Heat oil and saute onion and garlic. Add rice and cook for three minutes more, stirring constantly. Pour in hot water. Mix herbs and saffron in tomato sauce and season to taste. Pour onto rice, mix well, cover and simmer gently. Rice should be tender in about forty-five minutes. Add cheese a few minutes before rice is done. Serves six.

Spanish Rice

2 cups brown rice, cooked
1 onion, chopped
1 clove garlic, chopped
1 stalk celery, chopped fine
½ green pepper

¼ cup sesame oil
2 tablespoons tomato paste
2 tablespoons Parmesan
   cheese, grated
salt, paprika

In oil, saute onion, garlic, celery and green pepper for five minutes. Add cooked rice and more oil if necessary. Fry and turn rice until each grain is separated. Add tomato paste and continue to turn. Season to taste and serve with grated cheese. Serves six.

Vegetarian Loaf

½ cup brown rice
1 cup lentils
4 small onions, chopped
4 cloves garlic, chopped
2¼ cups water

few leaves of fresh spinach
juice of two lemons
sea salt
few cherry tomatoes

Cook rice and lentils separately. Brown onion and garlic in a skillet and add lentils and rice. Stir, adding water. Simmer on medium heat for forty-five minutes. When cooked, add chopped spinach and lemon juice, salt to taste. Before serving, garnish with cherry tomatoes. Serves four to six.

French Rice Casserole

2 cups brown rice, cooked
2 ounces butter
1 cup milk

a pinch saffron
seasonings
1 cup Swiss cheese, grated

Combine cooked rice, milk, butter, seasonings and half of the cheese. Turn into a casserole and sprinkle remaining cheese on top. Bake at 350° oven heat for thirty-five minutes.

Wild Rice

Basic Wild Rice

For one cup of wild rice use three cups of water or vegetable broth. Wash rice. Bring water or broth to a boil and pour it over rice. Stir, cover and let stand overnight to absorb liquid. Reheat to serve. Serves six.

Wild Rice with Mushrooms

½ cup wild rice
½ cup brown rice
1 pound fresh mushrooms
1 teaspoon celery flakes
½ teaspoon onion powder

½ teaspoon garlic powder
1 teaspoon nutritional yeast
3 cups water or broth
3 tablespoons Parmesan
   cheese, grated

Wash rice and cook in broth or water, with the seasoning and yeast in covered pan until water is absorbed and rice fluffy. Saute mushrooms in oil until tender. Mix with the rice. Serve with grated cheese on top. Serves four.

TWELVE

Grains and Cereals

Wheat

From the very early civilizations grain has formed the basis for mankind's diet. It is written in the Bible, "then God said, 'Behold, I have given you every plant yielding seed, that is on the surface of all earth and every tree which has fruits yielding seed, it shall be food for you.'"(Genesis 1:29-3.)

The so-called "Osiris grain" was discovered in an Egyptian tomb more than 3,500 years old where it was buried alongside a mummy. The grain was replanted in France and one seed produced 15 ears of wheat, which in turn yielded 600 more grains.

The majority of progressive nutrition schools recommends grains as complete foods. As long as the grain has not been treated with pesticides it can be eaten in its entirety. Almost every dish made with rice can also be made with wheat. The grain can be ground in an electric mill and after light cooking, may be eaten as cereal for breakfast, or the flour may be used to make bread. Grains can also be sprouted and served in salads.

Ann Wigmore of Boston, Massachusetts, known for her research and experimentation with wheat grain, is an enthusiastic advocate. She claims the sprouted wheat grain can be planted at home in good soil and the juice extracted when it reaches four inches in height to produce a healthful beverage.

To cook the whole wheat grains wash carefully and soak over-night. For one cup of wheat use four cups of water and simmer for two hours. Add more water if necessary. Eat like rice with butter, oil or sauce.

Eggless Pancakes—Crêpes Natures

½ cup whole wheat flour   3 tablespoons oil
1 teaspoon baking powder   3 tablespoons cold water
½ teaspoon salt

Sift dry ingredients and combine with oil and water. Beat with fork for a few minutes, adding more water if necessary. Let the dough set for ½ hour. Cook in a hot oiled skillet. Makes four pancakes.

Wheat Patties

½ pound wheat   1 tablespoon oil
1 onion, chopped   salt
2 tablespoons parsley,   water, as needed
  minced

Grind wheat. Add onion, parsley, oil, salt and enough water to make a thick dough. Mix well and allow to stand for two hours. Place a spoonful of the paste into an oiled pan. Spread to about ¼ inch thickness. Cook both sides until light brown. Serve with any green vegetables or with Broiled Tomatoes (page 69). Serves six.

Pap or Porridge (for infants)

If you prefer, grind the grains yourself in a cereal mill to make a flour. It is best to grind two or three times for young babies and then put it through a sieve. Good whole wheat flour may be purchased at your health food store or by mail.

Put two tablespoons of flour into a saucepan with a small amount of cold water and blend. Add boiling water while stirring constantly on low heat. The pap will be ready in minutes. Add milk, brown sugar or honey to taste.

Oats Porridge

1 cup rolled oats   2 cups water

Cover the oats with cold water, bring to a boil and cook for ten minutes over low heat. Salt or sweeten to taste. Oats may be cooked in milk also. For best nutrition it is better not to use *quick cooking* cereals.

Cornmeal

To cook stone ground cornmeal, use three cups of water to one cup of cornmeal. Mix cornmeal in a small amount of cold water to make a thin paste. Pour into boiling water and simmer ten minutes over very low heat, stirring constantly. Add butter or cream.

Buckwheat

You can buy buckwheat whole or split; the latter cooks faster. It is also available in the form of flour.

Kasha à la Russe

1 cup buckwheat, whole   1 egg
   grain   salt, butter and water

Place buckwheat in ungreased pan. Add egg and mix well. Cook over low heat stirring constantly until each grain is coated and separated. Cover with boiling water and add salt and butter. Cover and cook about forty to forty-five minutes over low heat, adding water every five minutes if necessary. Serve like rice. Serves six.

Buckwheat Grits

1 cup split buckwheat   2 cups water
salt, butter or cream

To make cereal, bring water to a boil and add buckwheat slowly, stirring constantly. Add water if necessary, and cook about ten minutes. Season to taste. Top with heavy cream or sour cream. Serves six.

Buckwheat Pancakes—Crêpes de Sarrasin

1 cup buckwheat flour   ½ cup milk
3 teaspoons baking powder   ½ cup water
salt   1 tablespoon oil or
½ teaspoon sugar   melted butter

Sift buckwheat flour, baking powder, salt, and sugar. Stir in liquids and blend well. Add oil and stir. Place in a warm spot to rise about one hour. Drop by the spoonful onto a very hot pan or skillet, spreading to make the crepe very thin. Turn and cook both sides. Serve with fruit or vegetables topped with maple syrup.

Granola Breakfast

½ cup wheat flakes   2 tablespoons raw sugar
½ cup oat flakes   dash of cinnamon
¼ cup toasted peanuts

Spread grains on a cookie sheet and place in 350° oven, turning often, until toasted. Then mix with peanuts, sugar, and cinnamon. Serve with milk and fresh fruit in season. Serves two.

Seed and Nut Breakfast

¼ cup millet
¼ cup sunflower seeds
¼ cup pumpkin seeds
1 ounce filberts

1 ounce walnuts
2 tablespoons raw sugar
  or honey
apple or pear

Grind millet first, then grind seeds and nuts. Mix ingredients together with sugar or honey, adding a fresh apple or pear. Serve with milk or cream. Serves two.

THIRTEEN

Miscellaneous Dishes

Gnocchi

1 cup milk	4 tablespoons Parmesan
1 cup water	cheese, grated
½ cup farina	2 ounces butter
salt	bread crumbs

Scald milk and water. Just before boiling point, sprinkle in farina, stirring constantly to avoid lumps. Add cheese, saving small amount for garnish, salt and butter, cook until thickened. Pour into wet, shallow pan, smooth the top and chill. Cut into squares, dip in bread crumbs and place on oiled baking sheet. Top with grated cheese. Bake in 400° oven until brown. Serves four.

Variation: You can make the same dish, using cornmeal instead of farina. Serve with Tomato Sauce (page 37).

Carmelite Corn Crisp

1 cup white cornmeal	2 tablespoons corn oil
½ teaspoon salt	½ cup water
1 teaspoon sugar	½ cup milk

Combine the cornmeal, salt, sugar, and oil. Add water and milk and mix well. Spread the batter very thin on oiled cookie sheets. Bake in hot oven until crisp, then cut in squares and sprinkle with sugar.

Polenta

To make a good polenta, you should buy a finely ground corn-meal. You will find it in Spanish stores or in the Spanish section of a supermarket. It is called *harina de maiz, fina.*

Use one cup of water and two tablespoons of cornmeal per serving. Heat water in a saucepan, and sprinkle in the cornmeal with one hand, stirring constantly with the other. Bring to a boil and cook at medium heat continuing to stir for two minutes. Add water if necessary. The meal should have the consistency of mashed potatoes. Add butter and seasonings. Serve hot. Polenta can be topped with tomato sauce, tomato stew, or other vegetables.

Cornmeal Soufflé

4 cups milk	*2 ounces butter*
8 tablespoons cornmeal	*2 eggs*

Heat milk. Stir cornmeal into small amount of cold water to make smooth paste first and then add to milk. Cook until smooth, stirring constantly, or cook over double boiler. When cooked, add butter and egg yolks. Beat egg whites and fold in gently. Pour into an oiled baking dish and bake in moderate oven for about thirty minutes. Serves four.

Baked Macaroni

1 pound whole wheat or soy macaroni	*1 pint half and half*
	4 ounces butter
4 quarts boiling water, salted	*1 cup Parmesan or Swiss cheese, grated*

Cook macaroni in rapidly boiling water, twelve to fifteen minutes until tender. Add one glass of cold water, cover and let stand a few minutes before draining. Add half and half, butter, cheese and seasoning to taste. Mix well and pour into oiled casserole. Top with more grated cheese and bake at 350° about forty-five minutes or until a light brown crust forms on top. Serves six.

Swiss Cereal

1 cup oat flakes
1 cup water
¼ cup raisins
¼ cup dried apples

¼ cup chopped almonds
2 teaspoons raw sugar
1 teaspoon wheat germ

Soak oats overnight in water. Add other ingredients and serve with milk or cream. Serves four.

Seed and Fruit Breakfast

1 cup oat flakes
1 cup water
1 tablespoon wheat germ
¼ cup sesame seeds

¼ cup sunflower seeds,
    hulled
¼ cup raisins
few prunes, soaked
    overnight

Soak oat flakes overnight in water. Add other ingredients and serve with honey and sliced banana, or fresh fruits in season. Serves four.

Vegetable Nut Loaf

2 carrots
6 mushrooms
2 stalks celery
1 beet
2 large potatoes
2 onions
3 cloves garlic
1 teaspoon thyme
1 teaspoon basil
1 teaspoon parsley

1 teaspoon salt
1 cup toasted or fresh bread
    crumbs
3 tablespoons grated cheese
1 teaspoon nutritional yeast
½ cup vegetable juice
2 tablespoons sunflower
    meal
2 tablespoons chopped
    walnuts
1 tablespoon sunflower oil

Grind vegetables very fine. Combine all ingredients and knead well. Form into loaf and place into oiled, shallow baking pan. Bake at 350° for fifty minutes. Serves four.

Stuffed Cabbage with Couscous (Chou Nature à l'Étouffée)

1 white cabbage
1 small pumpkin, peeled
2 tablespoons oil
2 onions, chopped
1 shallot, chopped

1 clove garlic, chopped
juice of one lemon
salt to taste
couscous: cook separately in
  salted water

Wash leaves and heart of cabbage and cut into strips as for sauerkraut. Cut pumpkin into small chunks. Into cookware, place oil, onions, garlic, shallot, pumpkin and cabbage. Cover tightly and cook on low heat about forty-five to fifty minutes. When tender, add salt and lemon juice. Serve with couscous. Serves four.

French Crêpes

The French claim the first crêpe (pancake) was made in France, the Chinese in China, the English in England, and so forth. According to legend, when the future Queen Ann was a country girl, a prince stopped at her door asking for a meal. She had nothing more than a little flour and an egg, and with it she made a small flat cake which became known as a crêpe. The prince, impressed by her beauty, married her. Because she was a country girl, she was called "La reine en sabots," the queen in clogs.

French Crêpes

3 eggs, well beaten
1 cup flour, sifted

½ cup milk or water
salt

Combine the eggs and flour. Slowly add water or milk and salt. Beat until very smooth, adding more water to it if necessary. The batter must not be too thick. Oil a heavy skillet. Put in a small amount of the batter, tilting pan to spread and fry until light brown. Turn and cook the other side. Serves six.

Mushroom Crêpes

½ pound mushrooms, sliced
2 tablespoons oil
2 tablespoons sour cream

1 tablespoon chives,
  chopped
salt and pepper

Saute mushrooms in oil for five minutes allowing juice to evaporate. Add sour cream, chives and seasoning. Put a spoonful of filling on a crêpe and roll. Will fill two crêpes. Serve immediately.

Variation: Use Tomatoes Provencale, (page 70), or sauteed zucchini for filling.

Crêpes Suzette

Make crêpe batter, using butter instead of oil, and sugar instead of salt. Fill with marmalade, roll, and sprinkle with sugar. Serve for breakfast with maple syrup.

Quiche Vegetarian

Originally, the quiche came from Lorraine, made with eggs, ham, and bacon. However, there is an easy way to prepare a quiche for a vegetarian meal.

2 8" pie crusts
2 packages of frozen spinach
½ pint heavy cream

3 eggs
1 teaspoon flour
2 tablespoons grated Swiss
  cheese

Buy frozen pie crusts at supermarket or make them yourself. Cook spinach slightly and drain. In a bowl combine cream and eggs, add spinach, and flour. Mix thoroughly. Pour into pie crusts. Top with the cheese. Bake in preheated oven at 350° to 400° about thirty minutes, or until golden brown.

You can vary this recipe by using broccoli, chopped asparagus, or mushrooms in place of spinach. Serves six to eight.

Vegetarian Egg Rolls

Buy ready-made egg roll dough in ethnic section of supermarket or Oriental food store.

½ pound soy oil
1 small white cabbage
3 stalks celery
1 onion

3 carrots
¼ pound bean sprouts
dough for six egg rolls

In a skillet lightly saute the vegetables in a small amount of oil, turning constantly. When ready, place three or four tablespoons of this mixture in the center of each rectangle of dough and roll, folding ends in to enclose filling. Let rest for a short while, then deep fry in the remaining oil. Serve hot, two egg rolls per person. Serves three.

Yogurt

Originally yogurt came from Bulgaria, where the people are said to live to a very old age due to eating sour milk.

The culture which makes yogurt is called *lacto bacillus bulgaricus*. You can buy it at a health food store or pharmacy, and make your own yogurt. However the easy way to do it is to buy a plain, natural yogurt and save part of it.

Heat one quart of raw (unprocessed) milk until it is hot but not boiling. Pour it into small sterilized jars, adding ½ teaspoon of the saved yogurt to each jar and mix well. Place the jars in a shallow pan of warm water, and cover with a wool cloth to keep it warm. Allow to stand overnight. Put lids on jars and store in refrigerator.

Don't forget to set aside a small quantity of *this* yogurt for the next batch.

Pizza Provençale

Crust:

¼ cup unbleached flour

2 tablespoons baking
  powder

½ cup oil

4 tablespoons chilled water

Filling:

4 large tomatoes, skinned,
  and cooked to a heavy
  puree

2 cloves garlic, chopped

6 black olives

½ teaspoon basil

1 tablespoon olive oil

½ teaspoon thyme

½ teaspoon oregano

Mix flour, salt, and oil and work dough with a fork. Sprinkle water over it, one spoonful at a time. Dough should be stiff. If not, add more flour. Form a ball and roll out in circle on flour covered board. Fit into eight inch pie pan and spread with tomato puree, garlic and olives. Sprinkle with oil and herbs. Bake in pre-heated over 450° for twenty-five minutes.

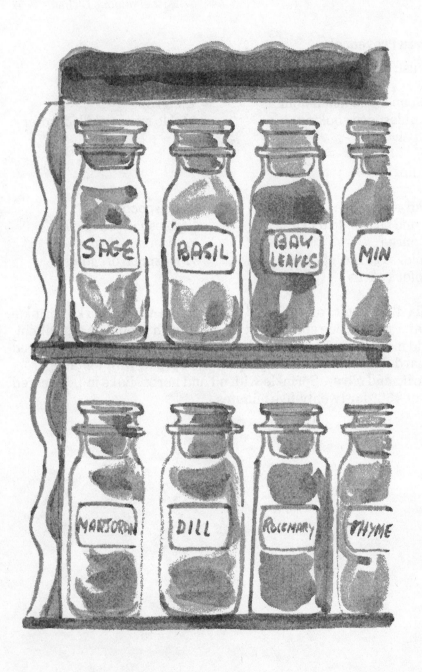

FOURTEEN

Cheeses

There are many varieties of cheeses. France produces the most and the best known cheeses, such as Brie, Camembert, Port Salut, Pont l'Eveque, Roquefort and many others. Well known Italian cheeses include Parmesan, Romano, Provolone, Bel Paese and Mozzarella. Swiss cheese is very popular, as is English Cheddar. Cheeses furnish the body calcium, vitamin B_2 and protein. The hard cheeses such as Parmesan, Provolone, Swiss, Cheddar and Romano are good for cooking in casseroles and sauces. Soft cheeses such as Brie, Camembert, Limburger, and semi-soft cheeses like Muenster, Tilsit, and Blue, are used in sandwiches. Cheeses are suitable for main dishes, sauces or spreads and in salads. Always melt cheese in double boiler rather than over direct heat.

Cream cheese, cottage and farmer's cheese are very good with fruit, compote, and green salad. Feta, Cheddar and Roquefort are used in tossed green salad or vegetable salad. It is considered a continental delicacy to serve fresh fruit with assorted cheeses. For example: apples with a piece of Provolone or Swiss; or pears with a piece of Bel Paese or Gouda.

Coeur à la Crème

2 ounces of cream cheese
2 tablespoons sour cream

1 tablespoon sugar
1 tablespoon milk

Mix cream cheese and milk in bowl. Add sour cream and sugar and beat with a fork until smooth. Pack into a wet, heart shaped mold and chill for one hour. Unmold and serve immediately or refrigerate. Serve with blueberries. Serves two.

Cottage Cheese with Herbs

1 pound cottage cheese
½ pound sour cream
2 tablespoons milk
1 sprig marjoram, chopped

2 sprigs parsley, chopped
2 tablespoons chives, chopped
1 sprig basil, chopped

Blend all ingredients in a bowl. Let stand for one hour before serving. Serves six.

Cheese Pancakes

Make crêpe batter (page 94). Pour a small amount of batter into buttered skillet and tilt pan to spread. Fry until light brown, turning to cook other side. Place spoonful of cottage cheese in center, fold and top with fruit sauce or preserves.

Cheese Croquettes

1 cup whole wheat or soy
  crumbs
1 cup Parmesan cheese,
  grated
1 cup Cheddar cheese,
  grated

salt
paprika
1 egg, beaten
2 tablespoons milk or
  half and half

Mix bread crumbs with grated cheese, salt and paprika. Add egg and milk. If batter is too thin, add more bread crumbs; if too thick, add more milk or water. Shape into croquettes and roll in bread crumbs. Fry in oil in hot skillet turning each side. Drain dry on absorbent paper. Serve with mashed potatoes or other vegetables. Makes six croquettes.

FIFTEEN

Eggs

If you do eat eggs, you can make many dishes with them and they are a good source of protein and iron for the body. Try to buy fertile eggs. They have more nutritional value. The yolk of a fresh egg should be dark yellow and the white should cling to the yolk.

Soft-Boiled Eggs

Cover eggs with water and bring to a boil. Lower the heat and boil for three minutes.

Hard-Boiled Eggs

Cover eggs with cold water and boil covered at low heat for ten to fifteen minutes. Plunge them into cold water and tap each end. Shells should then be easy to remove.

Poached Eggs

Heat water in a saucepan to boiling. Add salt and one tablespoon of vinegar. Break each egg gently into a cup, saucer, or egg poacher and slide it gently into water. Remove with perforated ladle, draining water carefully.

Eggs Daisy

Section a hard-cooked, shelled egg into six parts. Arrange in petal shape on a plate on lettuce leaves. Fill center with chopped black olives. Serve with Mayonnaise (page 28).

Eggs Sunny Side Up

If available use individual pottery baking dishes. Melt one teaspoon of butter per egg in dish. Break egg into it, being careful not to break yolk. Cook for one to two minutes over low heat until firm.

Eggs à la Russe

Slice hard-boiled eggs in half lengthwise. Carefully remove the yolk and mash it; mix with homemade Mayonnaise (page 28), (if using prepared mayonnaise, add mustard and lemon juice). Add a few capers and refill white with yolk mixture. Sprinkle with paprika and top with chopped chives or parsley.

Eggs Portuguese

Prepare hard-boiled eggs and cut lengthwise. Make a white sauce with milk, flour and butter, adding one tablespoon of tomato paste per cup of milk. Add seasonings and mix well. Add the eggs to the sauce and serve warm. Prepare one egg per serving.

Eggs Florentine

Prepare Creamed Spinach (page 68) and poach one or two eggs per serving. In individual ramekins or small casseroles make a bed of spinach. Add one slice of toasted corn bread and one or two poached eggs to each dish. Pour Sauce Blanche (page 34) over each and sprinkle with Parmesan cheese. Place under broiler for five minutes.

Eggs in Aspic

2 teaspoons vegetable
   gelatin
1 pint vegetable broth

1 tablespoon vinegar or the
   juice of one lemon
3 soft-boiled eggs, shelled

Dissolve and cook gelatin in strained, clear vegetable broth. Add one tablespoon of cider vinegar or the juice of one lemon. Pour into individual wet molds and add one egg to each. Chill. To unmold, dip each mold in warm water and invert on plate. Garnish with sprigs of parsley or watercress.

French Omelette (Basic)

Break eggs in a bowl (2 eggs per serving) and beat with a fork until blended. Add one teaspoon of water or milk per serving, salt and pepper and beat again. Pour into very hot, oiled skillet. As eggs cook at the sides, prick with a fork, so that the still soft egg mixture on top goes to the bottom of the pan. Don't overcook! While still moist, slide onto a platter, fold and serve hot.

Mushroom Omelette

Saute six mushrooms per serving in a saucepan. Add seasonings and chopped parsley. Prepare omelette. Spread cooked mushrooms over eggs and fold. Serve immediately.

Tomato Omelette

Fry sliced tomatoes in a skillet and remove to a side dish. Prepare omelette. When nearly done add sliced tomatoes and finish cooking. Fold and serve immediately.

Spanish Omelette

1 small onion, chopped
1 clove garlic, chopped
½ green pepper, chopped
1 teaspoon olive oil
½ cup tomato puree

½ cup water
1 teaspoon oregano
1 teaspoon basil
seasonings
6 eggs

Saute onion, garlic and pepper in oiled skillet. Add tomato puree, water, herbs and seasoning and let simmer for 15 minutes. Beat eggs. Make omelette and pour the sauce over it. Fold and serve. Serves four.

Sweet Omelette

Prepare omelette using milk and ½ teaspoon sugar per serving in place of pepper. Cook as usual. Fill with marmalade. Fold and sprinkle with sugar.

Omelette Flambée

Prepare sweet omelette without filling. When the omelette is ready, fold it and pour a small glass of rum or kirsch over it. Flame and serve.

Omelette Niçoise

1-2 tablespoons butter
2 tomatoes, cut in pieces
2 small zucchini, sliced
1 onion, chopped
1 clove garlic, chopped

8 eggs (two per serving)
salt and pepper to taste
1 teaspoon parsley, chopped
1 teaspoon fresh basil

Saute the vegetables, onion and garlic in butter until softened. For each serving, beat two eggs with a fork, adding a very small amount of water or milk, and seasoning. Cook eggs on high heat in buttered skillet. While cooking tip pan so center of egg runs to the side. While still moist, spoon some of vegetable mixture onto omelet, adding herbs, and fold. Serve immediately. Serves four.

Oeufs aux Fines Herbes

¼ teaspoon butter
1 egg
¼ teaspoon tarragon,
   dried
¼ teaspoon chives,
   dried

¼ teaspoon parsley, dried
   or fresh
salt, pepper or paprika
   to taste
shallow saucepan of boiling
   water

Butter the inside of an egg coddler. Beat egg with herbs and seasonings and pour into coddler. Cover tightly and stand coddler up to its neck in pan. Simmer for eight minutes. Serves one.

Eggs Country Style (Oeufs Paysans)

½ teaspoon butter
1 teaspoon chopped onions
1 teaspoon chopped
   mushrooms
1 egg

1 slice Swiss cheese,
   crumbled
salt and pepper to taste
shallow saucepan of boiling
   water

Saute onions and mushrooms briefly in ¼ teaspoon butter. Beat egg and add. Butter the inside of an egg coddler and pour in mixture. Season to taste and place cheese on top. Cover tightly and stand coddler up to its neck in pan. Simmer for ten minutes. Serves one.

SIXTEEN

Seeds and Nuts

Seeds and nuts are a most important source of vitamins, minerals, proteins and fats, all nutritionally essential for a vegetarian diet.

Sunflower Seeds Popular in Eastern Europe. Rich in vitamins A, B, and D, calcium, niacin, and protein, they can be eaten raw as a tasty snack or mixed with salads or vegetables. They are a good source of unsaturated fatty acid oil.

Pumpkin Seeds The American Indians have long enjoyed the seeds of pumpkin and squash. They contain calcium and magnesium and are good for snacks or mixed into salads.

Sesame Seeds Popular in the eastern part of the world, sesame seeds are used in pastry and candy. They contain a nutritious, valuable oil.

Pine Nuts *Piñons*, or better known as *pignoli*, are the edible seeds of various pines of the Pacific coast. Good as snacks, pine nuts can be mixed with fruits, salads, or baked in cookies and cake.

Almonds Popular in the Orient and Europe, almonds contain a milk and are rich in protein. Almond meal is used in confections, cake and cookies, and almond butter.

Hazel Nuts or Filberts Small nuts, easy to digest, filberts are frequently used in pastry.

Walnuts Originally from Persia, walnuts contain a rich oil.

Pecan Nuts A native of North America, pecans have a soft shell.

Brazil Nuts They are three sided and have a very hard shell.

Coconuts Tropical fruit of the coconut palm, they grow near the sea in soil rich in minerals. Their milk makes a healthy beverage and delicious desserts. Coconuts also provide an oil known as coconut butter.

Chestnuts Very popular in Central Europe, where they are sold roasted in winter time. They are used in vegetable dishes, cakes and desserts.

Cashew Nuts Imported from India, they must be roasted before being shelled. Rich in flavor.

Peanuts Peanuts are not nuts, but are related to the bean family. Rich in protein and fat, they produce a good oil. Peanuts are eaten roasted for a snack.

Pistachio Nuts The smallest nut, very tasty, is used in pastry, candy, and for ice cream flavoring.

Note: To remove the thin outer skin, pour boiling water over the shelled nuts and let stand ½ minute. Drain, and rub off the skin.

SEVENTEEN

Sprouts

The people of China have used sprouts for centuries and prepare them in many ways.

Sprouted seeds, grains, and beans are valuable foods, because they contain the elements to grow new plants. Sprouts can be grown indoors as well as out. The value of the sprouts depends on how they are grown and on the richness of the soil. Seeds for sprouting should be free from chemical treatment. Many seeds have been gassed and do not sprout! Do not buy the garden seeds available in nurseries or super markets; they are for planting, not for eating.

You can sprout:

Alfalfa—A small seed and probably the best for salad. Sprouts to two inches.

Mung Bean—The Chinese bean. Sprouts easily and grow to three inches in height.

Wheat—Be sure to have the right kind; many don't sprout.

Rice—With the germ still in it; may be found in Oriental stores.

Lentils—Have a sweet flavor but sprout only to one inch long.

Sunflower (unhulled)—They sprout rapidly.

Soy Bean—Must be cooked before eating.

Rye—May be served with cereal.

Directions for Sprouting

You can buy a commercial sprouting container, available in health food stores or by mail order. Or, you may use any clean container reserved just for sprouting. I use a glass pie plate, which is best for small seeds like alfalfa or parsley. A shallow pan may be better for beans and grains or a glass jar with a wide mouth will also do the job. Cover the mouth with cheesecloth and fasten with rubber band.

First: Clean and remove any broken seeds as they will not sprout and may ferment. Cover seeds with lukewarm well or spring water and soak overnight. Do not use distilled water as the seeds will not sprout. Drain off water and rinse. Place them in the container, cover and keep damp. For hard-shell beans or grains, cover with a damp cloth. Keep moist by rinsing the seeds three times a day. Small seeds should be ready in four or five days. Beans may take six to eight days.

Refrigerate sprouts as soon as they are ready in covered jars and use within a few days. Serve them raw in salads; they are also tasty sandwich fillers. Sprouts are sometimes mixed with bread dough or eaten with a cereal for breakfast. Mung bean sprouts can be added to any hot vegetable dish, a few minutes before serving.

Wheat Alfalfa Sandwich

Spread two slices of whole wheat bread with cream cheese. Cover with alfalfa sprouts and a slice of cucumber.

Nut Sprout Sandwich

Spread two slices of soy or corn bread with nut butter. Add a leaf of lettuce filled with sprouts and top with slice of tomato.

EIGHTEEN

Desserts

Gelatin Desserts

In the vegetarian diet, the jelling agents come from the sea: carrageen or Irish moss, and agar-agar. They have no food value and therefore can be used in low-calorie diets.

To thicken one cup of boiling liquid use one teaspoon of agar-agar powder or flakes (softened in cold liquid). Follow instructions of the kind you buy.

Basic Fruit Gelatin

½ cup cold fruit juice
2 teaspoons agar-agar
   powder

1½ cups hot fruit juice
¼ cup honey

Soften gelatin in cold juice. Add hot juice, honey and boil for one minute, stirring until dissolved. Add slices of fresh fruits. Mold or put in sherbet glasses. Chill. Serves four.

To unmold gelatin loosen the edge with *warm* knife, then dip mold in warm water and invert on serving dish.

Mocha Gelatin

1 cup strong coffee
4 teaspoons instant carob
3 tablespoons sugar

2 teaspoons agar-agar flakes
½ pint heavy cream

Dissolve the carob in coffee and add sugar. Heat the mixture in a saucepan to near boiling. Dissolve agar-agar in one tablespoon of cold water and pour into coffee mixture. Cook for three minutes stirring constantly. Let cool. Whip cream and fold into gelatin. Pour into mold and chill until firm. Unmold and top with ice cream or whipped cream. Serves four.

Cherries Delight

1 teaspoon gelatin
1 pint black cherry juice
1 tablespoon honey

10 fresh cherries
4 slices pineapple
few pignoli

Dissolve gelatin in small amount of cold water, mix with fruit juice and honey and cook over low heat for ten minutes. Add cherries and pour into individual sherbet glasses. Chill. Top with pineapple slice and pignoli. May be served with whipped cream or sour cream. Serves four.

Carob Coconut Gelatin

2 tablespoons instant carob
   powder
1 tablespoon raw sugar
2 tablespoons coconut meal

1 teaspoon gelatin
1 banana
1 cup milk

Combine ingredients, except gelatin, in blender until creamy. Cook gelatin in water. Add to mixture and blend again. Pour into sherbet glasses and chill. Top with slices of banana. Serves three.

Gelatin Hawaiian

1 can unsweetened pine-
    apple, sliced
3 tablespoons honey
1 pint fresh strawberries or
    raspberries

¼ cup pineapple juice or
    coconut juice
2 teaspoons agar-agar or
    other gelatin
2 tablespoons coconut meal

Open can of pineapple and set aside four slices. In blender, combine honey, berries, pineapple, coconut and juice for a few minutes. Soften gelatin in ½ cup cold water and bring to boil. Mix in blender with the fruits and blend again. Pour into individual sherbet glasses and add one slice of the remaining pineapple to each. Chill, garnish with berries on top and sprinkle with coconut meal.

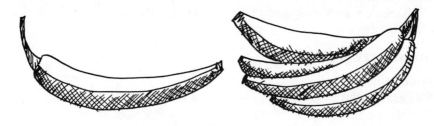

Banana Gelatin (Gélatine de Banane)

This gelatin can be made in ten minutes.

2 tablespoons instant carob
1 teaspoon Dutch cocoa
2 tablespoons raw sugar or
    honey
2 bananas
1 egg

1 cup milk
1 envelope unflavored
    gelatin
chopped cashew nuts
½ teaspoon vanilla extract
boiling water

Combine ingredients, except gelatin and nuts, in blender and mix until creamy. Dissolve gelatin, first in one tablespoon cold water, then in three tablespoons boiling water. Add to mixture in blender with vanilla and blend again. Pour into sherbet glasses and chill. Top with nuts. Serves two to three.

Custards

Custard Nadine

1 pint milk
3 eggs, beaten
2 tablespoons sugar
1 tablespoon vanilla

1 banana
2 ounces dates
2 ounces of chopped almonds
    and walnuts
½ pint cream

Warm milk and pour it over the beaten eggs. Return to pan and add sugar. Reheat gently until the mixture thickens, stirring continuously. Do not boil. Remove from heat and add vanilla. Peel and chop banana and mix with dates. Pour custard into four sherbet glasses, spoon the fruits over it and sprinkle with nuts. Chill. Serve with whipped cream. Serves four.

Strawberry Custard

l pint milk
3 eggs, beaten
1 tablespoon honey
1 tablespoon vanilla

1 pint fresh strawberries
2 ounces coconut meal
1 tablespoon sugar

Prepare as for Custard Nadine and mix the fruits with honey. Chill. Top with coconut meal.

Peach Cream Alexandra

3 eggs, beaten
1 pint milk
2 tablespoons sugar

2 tablespoons coconut meal
4 peaches, soaked in honey
1 teaspoon vanilla

Beat eggs. Scald milk and pour over the beaten eggs. Return to pan and add sugar and one spoon of coconut meal. Reheat the mixture, stirring constantly until thickened but do not boil. Remove from heat and cool. Peel and slice peaches and soak them in honey. Fill four sherbet glasses with half of the cream, then add the peaches, and cover with the rest of the cream. Sprinkle with remaining coconut meal. Top with peach-honey ice cream. Serves four.

Banana Custard (uncooked)

4 bananas
1 cup milk
2 tablespoons honey

2 tablespoons raisins
½ pint ice cream
1 teaspoon vanilla extract
few walnuts, chopped

Peel and slice bananas. Put them into a blender with enough milk to blend. Add honey, raisins, and ice cream and blend again. Pour into sherbet cups and put in freezer for ½ hour. Top with walnuts.

Apple Desserts

Apples Bonne Femme

6 baking apples
6 teaspoons sugar
2 ounces sweet butter

4 teaspoons honey
½ cup water

Wash and core apples leaving the skins on and place them in a shallow baking dish. In the center of each apple place a dot of butter and one teaspoon of sugar. Mix honey and water and pour over the apples. Bake in moderate oven for about forty-five minutes. Serve cold or hot. Top with sour cream or Fruit Sauce (page 34).

Apple Sauce (uncooked)

4 large apples
2 teaspoons lemon juice
4 dried apricots, soaked

¼ cup apple juice
¼ cup honey

Peel, core and slice apples. Pour lemon juice over them to prevent discoloration. Blend in blender with juice, honey, and apricots until smooth. Chill before serving.

Apple Meringue

2 pounds apples
2 tablespoons honey
1 tablespoon grated lemon
  rind

3 egg whites
2 tablespoons sugar

Cook cored and sliced apples in a very small amount of water. Mash or blend like apple sauce and add honey and grated lemon. Place into a baking dish. Beat the egg whites until stiff and fold in the sugar. Pile on top of apple sauce and spread to the edge of dish. Bake at 275° for about one hour until meringue is crisp and light brown in color. Serve warm or cold. Serves four.

Fried Apples (Pommes Frites)

1 cup unbleached flour,
  sifted
1 tablespoon baking soda
1 tablespoon sugar
2 eggs, well beaten

1 cup milk
1 tablespoon oil or
  melted butter
2 cooking apples

Mix flour, baking soda and sugar and beat with eggs. Gradually add milk and oil or butter. Pell, core and slice apples into small pieces. Add to batter and mix. Drop by the spoonful onto hot, oiled fry pan. Cook until golden brown on each side. Sprinkle with sugar. Serve hot.

Apple Almond Cream

4 apples
2 tablespoons apple juice
1 banana
1 tablespoon honey

2 tablespoons almond meal
2 tablespoons sour cream
½ teaspoon almond extract

Combine peeled apples, juice, banana, and honey in blender. When smooth add almond meal, sour cream, and extract and blend again for a few seconds. Pour into sherbet glasses and chill. Top with almonds. Serves four.

Puddings

Baked Pudding Hortense

⅓ cup white rice	2 egg yolks
1 quart milk	2 teaspoons vanilla
½ cup sugar	2 egg whites, beaten

Cook rice in milk and sugar, being careful not to overcook. When ready, pour into baking dish and add egg yolk and vanilla. Mix well. Fold in the stiffly beaten egg whites. Top with bread crumbs and sugar. Bake in moderate oven until light brown. Serve cold with Fruit Salad (page 34), or Carob Sauce (page 33). Serves four.

Raisin Pudding

1 quart milk	3 egg yolks
5 tablespoons farina	3 egg whites, beaten
½ cup raisins	bread crumbs and brown
2 teaspoons maple syrup	sugar to garnish

Heat milk to near boiling. Sprinkle farina in slowly, stirring constantly. When cooked a few minutes, add washed raisins, syrup, egg yolks and mix well. Beat the egg whites and fold into mixture. Pour into individual custard cups and sprinkle with bread crumbs and brown sugar. Bake at 325° until light brown. Serve hot or cold and top with Fruit Sauce (page 34), or Custard Sauce (page 33). Serves four.

Tapioca Pudding

2½ cups milk	3 tablespoons shredded
3 tablespoons minute	coconut
tapioca	1 egg, separated
3 tablespoons sugar	fruits in season

Combine milk, sugar, tapioca, coconut and the egg yolk in sauce pan and cook on low heat stirring constantly. Remove from heat when it begins to boil. Allow to cool. Beat the egg white stiff and fold it into the mixture. Pour into custard cups. Chill and top with fresh fruit. Serves four.

Carob Pudding

2 tablespoons unbleached
  flour
4 tablespoons carob powder
4 tablespoons sugar
3 cups milk

1 egg yolk
1 egg white, beaten
1 teaspoon vanilla extract
½ pint heavy cream

In a bowl combine flour, carob and sugar and mix with a small amount of cold water. Scald milk and pour it over the mixture. Add egg yolk, blend and cook, stirring constantly until creamy and smooth. Remove from heat, fold in the beaten egg white and vanilla. Pour into individual custard cups. Chill and top with whipped cream. Serves four.

Chestnut Pudding (Suprême de Marrons)

1 pound chestnuts
¼ cup milk
2 tablespoons sugar

1 teaspoon vanilla
½ pint heavy cream,
  whipped

Split the chestnuts around the head and immerse them in boiling water for a few minutes. The shell and skin should come off easily. If not, drop them in boiling water again.

Cook shelled chestnuts by starting in cold water for approximately one hour. When tender, mash them to make a very fine puree. Add warm milk, sugar and vanilla and beat thoroughly. Chill. Top with the whipped cream. Serves three or four.

Tapioca Cream

1 cup milk
1 cup water
3 tablespoons sugar

2 tablespoons minute
  tapioca
½ pint heavy cream
1 tablespoon vanilla extract

In a saucepan combine milk, water, sugar and tapioca and cook over low heat, stirring continuously. Remove from heat just as it begins to boil. Allow to cool. Whip the cream moderately and mix with the tapioca. Add vanilla and whip again until well blended. Serves two to three.

Blancmange

2 cups milk
2 tablespoons cornstarch

2 tablespoons sugar and
  honey
1 teaspoon almond extract

Scald milk. Mix starch and sugar in small amount of water and add to milk. Bring to a boil, stirring constantly, cooking for one to two minutes. Add almond extract. Pour into custard cups and chill. Top with fruits. Serves four.

Flan

5 eggs
5 ounces sugar
3½ ounces flour, sifted
2 cups warm milk

1 ounce melted butter
1 teaspoon vanilla extract
  or lemon peel

In a bowl, mix eggs and sugar together. Then slowly add flour. Dilute these ingredients with warm milk (not hot) and melted butter. Blend and add vanilla extract or lemon peel. Turn into an oiled mold and bake at 375° for about forty-five minutes. (A knife blade will come out clean when done.) Serves six.

Mousse

Strawberry Mousse (Mousse à la Fraise)

1 pint fresh strawberries,
  unsweetened
3 bananas
2 tablespoons honey

3 tablespoons fruit juice
  (cherry or berry)
2 tablespoons sour cream
4 walnuts

Wash strawberries and set aside four medium ones. Blend the rest of the berries with the bananas, honey, and juice. Add sour cream and blend again. Pour into sherbet glasses and chill. Garnish top with the remaining strawberries and walnuts. Serves four.

Carob Mousse

Carob candy may be bought at health food stores.

4 ounces carob chunks
2 ounces butter
1 tablespoon honey

2 tablespoons milk
1 teaspoon orange extract
½ pint heavy cream,
    whipped

Melt carob and butter with milk and honey in double boiler until mixture is blended. Allow to cool. Fold gently with extract into the whipped cream. Chill before serving. Serves four.

French Chocolate Mousse

4 ounces unsweetened
    chocolate
4 ounces butter
1 cup raw sugar

4 egg yolks
4 egg whites, whipped
4 tablespoons milk
2 tablespoons orange extract
    or liqueur

Melt chocolate in top of double boiler, add butter, sugar, and the egg yolk and beat until creamy and smooth. Let cool. Beat the egg white stiff, and fold in mixture. French cooks add kirsch or Cointreau liqueur instead of orange extract. Chill before serving. Remember it is very rich. May be used to top sponge cake or pound cake.

Miscellaneous

Pears Marie Antoinette

1 quart milk
¼ cup polished rice
¾ cup sugar
1 egg, beaten
1 teaspoon vanilla
4 fresh pears

2 cups water
1 teaspoon lemon peel
1 teaspoon chopped ginger
2 tablespoons red wine or
    apple cider vinegar

Cook rice in milk with ¼ cup of sugar. Combine water, ½ cup of sugar, lemon peel, ginger, and wine or vinegar and bring to a boil. Cook five minutes. Add the pears and simmer until tender. Let cool and pour over rice. Top with strawberry or cherry syrup. Serves six.

French Egg Snow (Oeufs en Neige)

4 eggs
3 cups milk

4 tablespoons sugar
1 tablespoon vanilla extract

First separate eggs and set the yolks aside. Beat the egg whites very stiff. Bring the milk and sugar to a boil and drop the egg whites, spoonful by spoonful, into the boiling milk. Let them cook one minute each. Place them on a plate to cool. They should each look like a small ball. To the same milk, add beaten egg yolks and vanilla and reheat mixture, stirring constantly, until it thickens. Do not boil. Remove from heat and pour into a bowl and top with the egg whites. They will look like small floating islands of snow. Serve chilled. Serves eight.

Cherries Jubilee

1 pound cherries, cooked
    and sweetened
1 pint vanilla ice cream

1 small glass of liqueur,
    Cointreau or cognac

Drain juice from cherries and warm in a saucepan. Add liqueur, and ignite with a match and wait until alcohol from the liqueur has burned off. Fill individual sherbet glasses with ice cream, pour the warm cherries over them. Serve immediately. Serves four.

Frozen Yogurt

½ pound berries or peaches
½ pint plain yogurt
2 tablespoons honey

Wash and crush berries with a fork, or, if using peaches, peel and cut into pieces before crushing. Add honey and mix together with yogurt. Pour into a container and freeze for several hours. Serves one or two.

Flamed Bananas (Bananes Flambées)

4 bananas
2 teaspoons sweet butter

2 tablespoons raw sugar
1 liqueur glass of rum

Cut bananas lengthwise and arrange in buttered baking dish. Sprinkle with sugar and bake in oven at 350°-400° until bananas are brown and soft. Sprinkle with rum, ignite and serve flaming. Can be topped with whipped cream or ice cream. Serves four.

Coconut Tahitian

3 egg yolks
4 tablespoons sugar
2 cups coconut meal

½ cup condensed milk
3 egg whites, beaten

Beat eggs yolks with sugar. Mix coconut meal with milk. Combine the two mixtures and fold in beaten egg whites. Pour the mixture approximately one inch deep, into an oiled cake pan. Bake at 325° for thirty minutes. Serve cold with slices of unsweetened pineapple. Serves four.

Cake with Cherries (Clafouti aux Cerises)

Clafouti is a cake, mixed with cherries or other fruit; made in the Limousin and Berri provinces of France.

⅔ cup flour, sifted
3 eggs beaten
1 cup milk

2 tablespoons sugar
1 tablespoon vanilla extract

Filling:

3 cups fresh Bing cherries
½ tablespoon kirsch or cognac

1 tablespoon sugar

Mix filling ingredients and let them rest. Make a batter with the flour, eggs, milk, and beat well. Add sugar, salt and vanilla and beat until smooth. Fill an oiled, shallow baking dish with half of the batter and bake for a few minutes. Pour the cherry filling over it and cover with the balance of the batter. Bake in moderate oven, 375°, for one hour. Serves four to six.

Kissel

Kissel is a Russian dessert, also made in Denmark, consisting of fruits and starch. Good for babies and the sick.

I prefer to use rice flour instead of starch; rice flour may be obtained in any store specializing in gourmet foods.

1 pint fresh strawberries or
  raspberries
2 tablespoons rice flour

1 tablespoon honey
1 banana
4 tablespoons whipped
  cream

Crush fruits in blender and strain to obtain a heavy but clear sauce. In a saucepan, dissolve flour in small amount of water and add fruit sauce. Cook over low heat, turning constantly. Add honey and mix well. Pour into individual sherbet glasses and chill. Top with slices of banana and whipped cream. Serves two to four.

NINETEEN

Pastry

It is not easy to make good pastry. It takes practice and experience.

From a nutritional viewpoint, we should not eat much pastry. Fruit pies are delicious to the taste, and better for health because the dough is lighter, less sugar is used, and the fruits are raw or slightly cooked.

Whole wheat flour is used more often in the vegetarian diet because it contains the whole of the grain, and is therefore a valuable source of nutrition. It contains more protein and minerals than unbleached white flour. *Never* buy bleached flour!

If you use whole wheat flour, however, it is more difficult to make pastry since it has a different, heavier texture. It is necessary to use more shortening and leavening and less flour.

Whole Wheat Pie Crust

1 cup whole wheat flour,
   sifted
1 teaspoon sea salt
2 tablespoons baking powder

4 ounces butter or vegetable
   butter
2 tablespoons cold water

Add the softened butter and work with a fork until mixture resembles bread crumbs. Add water, one spoonful at a time continuing to mix. Work the dough with your hands and form a ball. Place this on a large sheet of wax paper dusted with flour and place another sheet of paper on top. Roll the dough in this manner forming a circle of desired size. Peel off the top paper and invert your pie pan over it. Flip the paper over and pressing the pastry down into the pan, peel it from the crust. This method will help to hold the whole wheat pastry together.

Plum Filling:
Cut fresh Italian plums in sections removing the pits. Overlap them on pie shell and sprinkle with raw sugar or honey or both, depending on the sweetness desired.

Apple Filling:
Do the same with apples, adding 1 teaspoon of cinnamon. When the shell is filled, dot with butter or one tablespoon of heavy cream. You may also mix ¼ cup of cream with the yolk of an egg, beat and sprinkle over the fruit.

Bake at 425° for ten minutes, then lower heat to 375° for another twenty-five minutes.

Fresh Fruit Pie (Tarte aux Fruits Frais)

1½ cups unbleached white flour	salt
	dash of sugar
1 egg	4 ounces butter
lemon peel	2 tablespoons cold water

Sift flour onto board and make a valley in the center in which to drop egg, lemon peel, salt and sugar, mixing well. Add the softened butter and work with a fork. The dough must be smooth. If too stiff, add one tablespoon of cold water. Form ball, wrap in waxed paper and chill. Do not roll, but press into eight-inch pie pan. Fold edges and dot with butter. Place another pie pan on top of crust and bake in 375° oven for thirty to thirty-five minutes. Cool and fill with fresh strawberries, blueberries, sliced peaches or apricots. Cover the fruits with preserves and honey and top with whipped cream.

TWENTY

Cookies

Cream Cheese Cookies

8 ounces cream cheese
2 ounces butter
3 tablespoons sugar
1 cup unbleached flour

4 tablespoons milk
1 teaspoon vanilla extract
2 tablespoons raisins
2 tablespoons sesame seeds

Blend cheese, butter and sugar, working with a fork until smooth. Stir in flour, milk and vanilla. The dough should be stiff. It if is too thick, add water; if too thin, add more flour. Add raisins and shape into long rolls, two inches in diameter. Wrap in waxed paper and chill for one hour or more. Cut into thin slices and place on oiled cookie sheets. Bake at 400° oven heat for fiteen minutes. Sprinkle sesame seeds over warm cookies.

Vanilla Crescent Cookies

1 cup unbleached flour
3 ounces almond meal
¼ cup sugar

6 ounces butter
1 tablespoon vanilla extract
½ cup powdered sugar

Sift flour and almond meal together and add sugar, softened butter and vanilla. Dough must be stiff. If not, add more flour; if too thick, add water or milk. Chill. Roll into long, pencil-thin rolls on floured board. Cut into three-inch lengths and mold into crescents. Arrange on oiled cookie sheet and bake at 350° for twelve to fifteen minutes. *Caution:* The crescents break easily. When baked, roll them in powdered sugar.

Raisin Cookies

1 cup raisins
4 ounces butter
½ cup raw sugar
1 egg

2 cups sifted, unbleached
  flour
½ teaspoon salt
1 teaspoon vanilla extract

Rinse and drain raisins. Cream butter with sugar, add the beaten egg and mix well. Sift flour, add salt and blend into creamed mixture. Stir in vanilla with raisins. Drop by spoonsful onto oiled baking sheet. Bake in 400° oven about ten to fifteen minutes. Cool on baking pan. Makes about three dozen cookies.

Raisin Honey Cookies

¾ cup raisins
4 ounces butter
¼ cup brown sugar
1 egg
½ cup honey
1 teaspoon ginger

2 cups sifted, unbleached
  flour
½ teaspoon salt
1½ teaspoons baking
  powder
1 teaspoon cinnamon

Rinse and drain raisins. Cream butter with sugar, add beaten egg and mix well. Blend in the honey. Sift flour, salt and baking powder and add spices, blending into creamed mixture. Stir in the raisins. Drop by spoonsful onto oiled baking sheet. Bake in moderate 350° oven for fifteen to twenty minutes. Remove from baking pan to cool. Makes about three dozen cookies.

TWENTY-ONE

Confections

Chocolate Truffles (Truffes au Chocolat)

12 ounces unsweetened
  chocolate
6 ounces sweet butter
12 ounces sugar

2 egg yolks
2 teaspoons rum
2 ounces unsweetened Dutch
  cocoa

Melt the chocolate in a double boiler. The butter must be soft but not melted. Cream it in with the sugar, add egg yolks, and blend until the mixture is smooth. Fold in the warm chocolate, stirring constantly. Add rum and mix well. Chill over night in refrigerator. Roll a teaspoon of the mixture into a little ball and then roll in Dutch cocoa. Place each truffle on a paper doily.

Chestnut Truffles (Truffes aux Marrons)

1 pound chestnuts
6 ounces chocolate
1 teaspoon milk

6 ounces sugar
4 ounces sweet butter
2 ounces cocoa,
  unsweetened

Split the chestnuts along the round part and immerse them in boiling water for five minutes. Remove shell and skin. Cook them for one hour. When the chestnuts are tender, mash them into a very fine puree. Melt the chocolate in a double boiler, with one teaspoon of milk. Mix the chestnuts with chocolate, butter and sugar and blend. Chill overnight in refrigerator. Take one spoonful of the mixture and shape into small ball. Roll in cocoa. Put each truffle on a small paper doily.

Apricot Date Delight

12 apricots	*1 teaspoon orange peel*
18 dates	*1 tablespoon orange juice*
1 tablespoon honey	*4 tablespoons coconut meal*

Place apricots in ½ cup of cold water in saucepan and bring to a boil. Reduce heat and simmer for thirty minutes. Drain and crush apricots and dates. In a bowl, combine apricots, dates, honey, orange peel, and orange juice. Add the coconut meal and blend again. Shape into ball, roll in coconut meal. Cover with waxed paper and refrigerate for 24 hours before serving.

Stuffed Prunes

Wash large prunes and soak them in boiling water for fifteen minutes. While still warm, split them open and pit. Stuff each prune with a blanched almond or a cashew nut. Top with honey and roll in coconut meal.

Stuffed Dates

Make a paste of ground sunflower seed, sesame seed meal, honey, a few chopped almonds, and one or two tablespoons of orange or pineapple juice. Pit dates and stuff them with the mixture. Chill before serving.

Rose Hip Candy

Mix one tablespoon of rose hip jelly, which may be purchased at health food stores, with one teaspoon of sunflower meal. Form into a small ball and roll in sesame seeds. Chill before serving.

TWENTY-TWO

Beverages

Herb Teas

Herb teas are healthy and delicious. Try these different combinations.

Mix: 1 teaspoon of linden blossoms and 1 teaspoon of peppermint,

or, 1 teaspoon of papaya, one of mint and one of alfalfa,

or, 1 teaspoon of rose hips, one of mint and one of papaya,

or, 1 teaspoon of peppermint and one of orange blossoms,

or, 1 teaspoon of rose hips, one of mint, ¼ of hibiscus, 1 linden and spices.

Suitable spices for tea are: cloves, cinnamon, cardamon, ginger, lemon or orange peels. Brew in crockery or porcelain pot. Always use boiling water and let stand for two to five minutes.

Iced Herb Tea

4 teaspoons peppermint tea
1 teaspoon linden blossom
   tea

1 teaspoon rose hips tea
1 quart boiling water
¼ cup honey

Brew the teas. Cool. Add honey and serve in glass with a ring of fresh lemon, an ice cube, and a sprig of fresh mint.

Iced Tea

2 tablespoons English tea
2 tablespoons peppermint
   tea
1 quart boiling water

¼ cup honey
1 ring of fresh lemon per
   glass
dash of ginger

Serve chilled.

Iced Strawberry Tea

Two teaspoons of strawberry leaf tea to one pint of boiling water. Add one small cinnamon stick, the juice of one orange and ¼ teaspoon of orange peel. Serve chilled.

Fresh Mint Cooler

1 cup pineapple juice
2 tablespoons honey
1 orange, peeled and diced

1 cup mint tea, cooled
2 tablespoons cream

Put ingredients, except cream, into a blender, mix thoroughly. Add cream and blend again. Serve chilled with a sprig of fresh mint.

Party Punch

1 cup grape juice
1 cup pineapple juice
1 pint soda water
a few strawberries

1 small can unsweetened,
   crushed pineapple
sugar or honey, if desired

Mix the juices and water. Add fruits and serve chilled.

Nectar Punch

1 pint apple juice
½ pint water or ice cubes

½ pint apricot juice
1 orange

Mix the juices and water. Add one orange, sliced thinly. Sweeten as desired.

Carob Shake

A healthy nourishing beverage for children.

1 glass milk
1 tablespoon instant carob
1 teaspoon raw sugar

2 tablespoons natural honey
ice cream, available at
health food stores,
preferably carob flavor

Put milk, carob and sugar into a blender and mix for a few minutes. Add ice cream and blend again.

Vanilla Shake

8 ounces milk
1 tablespoon shredded
coconut
1 tablespoon raw sugar

1 teaspoon vanilla
2 tablespoons honey ice
cream, vanilla flavor

Mix milk, coconut, raw sugar and vanilla in blender. Add ice cream and blend another few minutes.

Banana Shake

8 ounces milk
1 egg yolk
1 tablespoon honey

1 banana
1 tablespoon shredded
coconut

Put all ingredients into a blender and blend at high speed.

Peach Yogurt Drink

2 peaches   1 tablespoon honey
1 cup apricot or peach juice   ½ cup yogurt

Put peaches, juice and honey in blender and mix thoroughly. Add yogurt, blend again for few seconds.

Carrot Shake

2 cups pineapple juice,   1 tablespoon honey
   unsweetened   1 tablespoon sesame seeds
1 medium carrot, diced   lemon wedges

Put juice and carrot into blender, cover and blend until carrot is liquefied. Add honey and sesame seeds and blend again. Serve cold with a wedge of lemon. Makes about three glasses.

Tomato Drink

2 cups tomato juice   1 sprig parsley
the juice of one lemon   1 sprig watercress
2 tablespoons sour cream   seasonings
                                   lemon wedges

Combine ingredients thoroughly in blender. Serve cold with a wedge of lemon. Makes about three glasses.

Almond Milk

2 cups water   ½ cup almonds, blanched
2 tablespoons honey

Blend ingredients in blender. Serves two or three.

Coconut Drink

2 cups warm water   *2 cups coconut meal*
2 tablespoons honey

Blend ingredients at high speed. Strain. Serve cold. Makes three
to four glasses.

Apricot Shake

½ pound dried apricots,   *1 cup milk*
* soaked overnight*   *2 tablespoons honey*
1 cup of the water in which   *1 tablespoon almond extract*
* apricots were soaked*

Blend all ingredients in a blender. Serve cold. Makes three
glasses.

Menus for Spring

BREAKFAST

Fruit of the Season
Whole Grain Cereal
Sanka, Tea or Herb Tea

LUNCH

Radishes with Peanut Butter
Grated Raw Carrots, with
   lemon juice
Cottage Cheese
Milk or Tea

DINNER

Apple Juice
Dandelion Salad with Beets
   and French Dressing
Asparagus, Sauce Polonaise
French Rice Casserole
Strawberry Mousse—
   Mousse à la Fraise
Peppermint Tea

BREAKFAST

Prune Juice
Pancakes with jelly
Carob Drink, or Herb Tea

LUNCH

Mushrooms in Green Sauce
Slice of Soy Bread with Cheese
Carrot Juice

BREAKFAST

Orange Juice
Poached Egg on Corn Bread
   toast
Coffee, Sanka, or Herb Tea

LUNCH

Vitality Salad
Fruit Compote
Milk or Tea

DINNER

Grape Juice
Carrot-Raisin Salad
   with Mayonnaise
Boiled Potatoes—en Robe de
   Chambre
Petit Pois à la Française
Cherries Delight

BREAKFAST

Grapefruit Juice
Farina
Milk, Sanka, or Tea

LUNCH

Hollywood Salad
   with slice of Soy Bread
Banana Shake

141

DINNER

Tomato Juice
Salade Parisienne
Vegetables Primavera
Wheat Patties
Carob Pudding
Papaya—Mint Tea

DINNER

Vegetable Juice
Celery, Olives, and Carrots,
    with lemon juice
Pipérade
Strawberry Custard
Iced Strawberry Tea

Menus for Summer

BREAKFAST

Fig Juice
Yogurt with fruit or honey
Zwieback with Preserves
Cafe au Lait, Sanka, Tea or
    Herb Tea

BREAKFAST

Fresh Peaches
Cold Whole Grain Cereal
Coffee or Tea

LUNCH

Cheese Pancakes
Morning Salad
Carob Shake

LUNCH

Tomatoes Vie Claire
Blue Cheese Spread with
    Crackers
Tomato Juice

DINNER

Cantaloupe
String Beans Mignonette
Grandma s Stuffed Tomatoes
Blancmange
Iced Tea

DINNER

Watermelon
Tossed Green Salad
Ears of Fresh Corn
Tomatoes Provençale
Peach Crème Alexandra

BREAKFAST

Orange Juice
Familia Cereal
Sanka with Warm Milk

BREAKFAST

Fruit Juice
Sour Cream with
    Blueberries
Tea or Herb Tea

LUNCH

Tartar Soup
Coeur à la Crème
Milk

DINNER

Honeydew Melon
Tomato Salad,
   Vinaigrette Dressing
Cucumber Salad,
   Vinaigrette Dressing
Stuffed Eggplant Creole
Pears Marie Antoinette
Iced Peppermint Tea

LUNCH

Minute Borscht
Cottage Cheese with Herbs,
Rye Crackers
Iced Tea

DINNER

Melon Surprise
Salad of the Auvergne
   Region
Cheese
Tapioca Pudding, topped
   with Fresh Peaches
Fresh Mint Cooler

Menus for Fall

BREAKFAST

Orange Juice
Fried Apples
Coffee, Tea or other
   Beverage

LUNCH

Lentil Salad with
Slice of Whole Wheat Bread
Carob Shake

DINNER

Grapefruit
Tossed Green Salad
Eggs Florentine
Apple Meringue

BREAKFAST

Fig Juice
Egg Sunny Side Up,
   with Toasted Oatmeal Bread
Coffee, Tea, or other
   Beverage

LUNCH

Avocado Vie Claire
Apple Sauce
Herb Tea

DINNER

Endive and Watercress
   Salad
Potée Brumaire with Soy
   Patties
Apple Almond Cream

BREAKFAST

Orange Juice
Buckwheat Grits
Coffee, Sanka or Tea

LUNCH

Nut Sprout Sandwich
Banana Shake

DINNER

Potpourri Salad
Broccoli with Sauce Polonaise
Potato Croquettes
Apple Bonne Femme
Spiced Tea

BREAKFAST

Prune Juice
Corn Meal, with Butter
Coffee or Tea

LUNCH

Onion Soup
Cheese with Pear
Milk or Coffee

DINNER

Grapefruit
Cole Slaw Naturel
Artichoke Florentine
Raisin Pudding

Menus for Winter

BREAKFAST

Dried Fruit Compote
Oatmeal cooked with Milk
Sanka, Coffee, or Tea

LUNCH

Vegetable Soup
Wheat-Alfalfa Sprout
    Sandwich
Tea

DINNER

Grapefruit
French Salad with
    Vinaigrette Dressing
Cauliflower au Gratin
French Chocolate Mousse

BREAKFAST

Prune Juice
Buckwheat Pancakes
Cafe au Lait

LUNCH

Spanish Soup
Cheese Omelette
Warm Beverage

DINNER

Fresh Fruit Salad
Red Cabbage Salad, with
    French Dressing
Vegetarian Gratiné
Kissel

BREAKFAST

Apricot Compote
Soft-Boiled Egg
French Toast

LUNCH

Potato Pancake with
    Apple Sauce or Sour Cream
Hot Coffee, or Milk

DINNER

Fantasia Salad
Spanish Rice
French Egg Snow

BREAKFAST

Morning Salad
Polenta with Light Cream
Warm Beverage

LUNCH

Grilled Cheese Sandwich
Fruit Compote
Milk

DINNER

Tomato Juice
Russian Salad
Wild Rice with Mushrooms
Prunes à la Grecque

Index

BOOKS OF RELATED INTEREST

THE GREENGROCER COOKBOOK by Joe Carcione provides the first seasonal arrangement of fresh fruit and vegetable recipes, with special chapters featuring exotic varieties. TV's Greengrocer has won "the trust and confidence of countless shoppers." — *TV Guide.* 252 pages, soft cover, $4.95.

In **THE EGG BOOK,** Robert and Gayle Allen offer more than a cookbook. Here is a primer, as well as a discussion of the history, art and cuisine of eggs. Available and eagerly accepted, eggs go with anything and this book is for the novice as well as the experienced cook who is searching for variety. 192 pages, soft cover, $4.95.

THE HERBAL DINNER: A RENAISSANCE OF COOKING by Rob Menzies is a unique, illustrated guide to understanding and using nature's herbal bounty as nourishment for the body, mind and soul. 224 pages, soft cover, $5.95.

THE COMPLETE BOOK OF GINSENG by Richard Heffern is an in-depth discussion of Asiatic and North American varieties including germination, cultivation, collection and medical preparation. 128 pages, soft cover, $3.95.

THE COMPLETE RECREATIONAL VEHICLE COOKBOOK by Robert and Gayle Allen is the only comprehensive cookbook for the millions who cook with limited facilities and minimum space in campers, vans, motor homes, sailboats and the back of the family station wagon. 204 pages, soft cover, $4.95.

THE ULTIMATE SOUP BOOK by Mike and Mary Spencer is truly the last word in soup books. Here are soups from the freezer, from the pantry, from the barnyard and from the sea presented in a delightful and witty format, cold fruit soups to pick-me-up lunches on hot summer days. 128 pages, soft cover, $4.95.

Available at your local book or department store or directly from the publisher. To order by mail, send check or money order to:

Celestial Arts
231 Adrian Road
Millbrae, CA 94030

Please include $1.00 for postage and handling. California residents add 6% tax.